Speaking
of
Christ

Speaking of Christ

A Lesbian Feminist Voice

CARTER HEYWARD

Edited by
Ellen C. Davis

THE PILGRIM PRESS
NEW YORK

"Ahead of Her Time, Yet Fully in It" appeared originally in *Christianity and Crisis*, September 14, 1987. Copyright *Christianity and Crisis*, 537 W. 121 Street, New York, NY 10027. Reprinted with permission.

"Naming Evil for What It Is" and "To Comfort Those Who Mourn" are reprinted by permission of *The Witness* magazine, Episcopal Church Publishing House.

Lyrics from "Hay Una Mujer Desaparecida" © 1978 Hereford Music. Used by permission of Redwood Records, Emeryville, California.

"Doing Feminist Liberation Christology," excerpted from *Lift Every Voice*, edited by Susan Brooks Thistlethwaite and Mary Potter Engel. Copyright © 1990 by Harper & Row Publishers, Inc.

Biblical quotations, unless otherwise noted, are from the Revised Standard Version of the Bible, copyright 1946, 1952, © 1971, 1973 by the Division of Christian Education of the National Council of the Churches of Christ in the U.S.A., and are used by permission. Any alterations are consistent with *An Inclusive Language Dictionary*, copyright © 1987 Division of Education and Ministry, National Council of the Churches of Christ in the U.S.A.

Library of Congress Cataloging-in-Publication Data

Heyward, Carter.
    Speaking of Christ : a lesbian feminist voice / Carter Heyward ; edited by Ellen C. Davis.
        p.   cm.
    ISBN 0–8298–0829–9
    1. Feminist theology.   2. Lesbianism—Religious aspects—Christianity.   3. Heyward, Carter.   I. Davis, Ellen C.   II. Title.
BT83.55.H48   1989
230'.082—dc20   89–35064

The Pilgrim Press, 475 Riverside Drive, New York, N.Y. 10115

Dedicated to
Anne E. Gilson
and others
who have spoken

Contents

Preface

Speaking of Christ. . . . He was a prophet though he said his work was that of a pastor: a pastor who, like a good shepherd, loves all who are committed to his care, rich and poor alike, those at the center of our civil and religious organizations as well as those left at the margins of society. This man believed that God is love and that in God's image we are created to respect and advocate the well-being of all sisters and brothers. He believed that love involves feeding the hungry, clothing those who are naked or cold, and providing access to education, employment, and health care to everyone. He believed that these conditions for a decent life are basic human rights and that they are the will of God.

He said that in difficult situations in which people must decide what is right, we must choose to obey the law of God rather than human laws that preclude love. He preached that the young people of his country should lay down their arms and refuse to fight on the side of their own government, which was oppressing the poor who struggled for bread and justice.

In this way Salvadoran Archbishop Oscar Arnulfo Romero incurred the wrath of the military and economic powers behind the puppet government of El Salvador. On March 24, 1980, Archbishop Romero was shot and killed as he was celebrating Mass in the Chapel of the Divine Providence in San Salvador.

What does this call forth in us? What in us is moved by occasions of suffering for justice, indeed, of more than suffering—of standing to be counted, of acting in solidarity with those who struggle for survival and poetry, and, if we are among the oppressed, of speaking and struggling for ourselves? These are christological questions because they draw us

9

toward the heart of humanity, that sacred place in which we not only meet the divine but are in some sense joined with God.

And the questions press on. Why are those whose lives reflect brilliantly the passion of God usually dismissed or despised by those who hold the power in place? Why are such people often marked for rejection, persecution, or death? Why is it that "humankind cannot bear very much reality" (T. S. Eliot), especially if the reality is goodness and love? Why do we kill our prophets, frequently the very people toward whom we are most drawn by a power we cannot name easily?

Do we not love and fear the freshness of those who call us to live rather than to stagnate, to grow into our full spiritual stature rather than to settle for a shallow mediocrity of ourselves? Do we not often flee, deny, and reject the people who might be lifelines for us, were we to accept their invitation to join them as friends in shaping together a sacred future?

Like the story of Archbishop Romero, these questions are christological: they are about what we love, how we love, whom we love, and about what we refuse to love. They are about fear, denial, violence, and about courage, risk, and peace. They are questions about power-over, that is, power exercised as control, and about power-with, that is, power as creative relational energy. They are about how we touch among ourselves what is most fully human and most fully divine.

These questions are by no means uniquely "Christian." They are basic, however, to a Christian commitment to justice and peace, to helping to bring forth that righteousness which rolls down "like an ever-flowing stream" (Amos 5:24b) and the "peace . . . which passes all understanding" (Phil. 4:7). This volume has been compiled in the spirit of this commitment.

This book is not in a classical or formal sense a "christology." With the exception of the first essay, which is an explicitly christological exploration, it is a collection of prose and homilies meant to evoke christological sensibilities—experiences, beliefs, and images of who or what "Christ" is, or may mean, for the reader. The pieces, composed over four years (1984–1988) for various occasions, were selected for that purpose. As I speak in each of the human commitment to justice and compassion, I literally am speaking of Christ.

Nor is this book *about* lesbianism or feminism. The subtitle, "A Lesbian Feminist Voice," is a means of signaling for the reader my sense of primary accountability: Who are my people? For whom, primarily, am I speaking and writing? It is also a way of lifting up and making visible particular dimensions of who I am which the dominant powers in the world and church would prefer be kept invisible. It is important to me that the reader know that this person who is speaking of Christ is a lesbian and a feminist who wants her readers to have this information.

At this moment in United States history, a largely reactionary church and state as well as progressive movements are attempting to keep lesbians and gaymen in the closet and to mute the radical implications of genuinely feminist voices. In this context, it is critical that we who can (we who have access to publishers, for example) simply speak the words, "I am lesbian. I am feminist." The words I speak—whether about grocery shopping, Anglican spirituality, sex, or Christ—are lesbian feminist words because I speak them.

To speak this truth is also a matter of authority and revelation—of giving embodied sensual, audible, and visible power to the real presence of lesbian feminist women in the churches, synagogues, and elsewhere. We are present. And we who are Christian speak of Christ.

Ellen Davis, my student and research assistant at the Episcopal Divinity School for several years, shares the commitment in which this volume is offered. A gifted lesbian feminist theologian and minister, Ellen also has a sharp editorial eye. It was she who took the initiative in selecting the materials for the book, brought order out of what seemed chaos, and finally edited them. Without Ellen the manuscript that was to become this book would have remained on the storage shelf of my office for quite some time. Working alongside Ellen, Carol Blanchard typed much of the manuscript. I am grateful to them both.

Marion Meyer, formerly Senior Editor at Pilgrim Press, encouraged this collection, contributing her characteristically good-humored insights to this task. Upon Marion's retirement, Stephanie Egnotovich inherited the project and led us toward publication in a spirit of fresh enthusiasm.

The completion of the book converged with a process of soul-searching in my life. During this time, several folks provided especially critical support for me and, thus, for the manuscript: Ann Briley, Mary Glasspool, Sydney Howell, Peg Huff, Jan Surrey, and my special companion Beverly Harrison each added more to the shape of this volume than they can know. To each and all, my thanks.

CARTER HEYWARD
Cambridge

1.

Doing Feminist Liberation Christology

Moving Beyond
"Jesus of History" and "Christ of Faith":
A Methodological Inquiry*

The master's tools will never dismantle the master's house. They may allow us temporarily to beat him at his own game, but they will never enable us to bring about genuine change. [1]

It is my thesis here that the historical doctrinal pull between Jesus of Nazareth and Jesus Christ, the human Jesus and his divine meaning, is no longer, if it ever was, a place of creative christological inquiry. Worse, it is a distraction from the daily praxis of liberation, which is the root and purpose of Christian faith. I should back up and explain that this thesis is the result of both my own work on this essay for the past two years and an ongoing dialogue throughout this same period with a number of other womanist and feminist Christian theologians of liberation. [2]

This essay began in the summer of 1986 in a paper I was to present at the American Academy of Religion. The paper was to focus on the debate between "the historical Jesus" and "the eternal Christ" as primary locus of christological inquiry. I began to prepare the paper on the hunch that the Jesus-of-history apologists, as much as their Christ-of-faith counterparts, tend to present as simplistic and one-dimensional that which can be experienced only in the angles and contours of bold relief. [3]

My interest was not primarily in constructing a christology but in pruning away some of the tangle of christological clutter to see what might be found underneath. I began this process by looking at two classical christological assumptions. The first was that "humanity" and "divinity" signify two discrete, objective "qualities" of what we can know and love, and that we come to know these qualities as polarities, or opposites. There can be no shared ground between the two. What we humans are, God is not, and vice versa: Human beings, for example, die; divine being does not.

The second assumption I examined was that christology is the study of how Christians understand these opposites, humanity and divinity, joined in the person of Jesus, thereby making him the Messiah or Christ to whom Hebrew Scriptures refer.

It seemed to me initially that the pendulum swing between Jesus of history and Christ of faith has continued historically to reflect a vitality in theological movement whereby one cannot become too smug about any given theological persona or period, or stuck in a particular christological dogma.[4]

Once I began wrestling with this study in a class of Christian feminists in the fall of 1986, however, I realized that the tension between the Jesus-of-history and Christ-of-faith poles in christological development reflects less a vitality than an obscurity. It obscures the troublesome dualism between divinity and humanity in which christology originated. This dualism continues to shape the dominant forms of Christian faith and praxis to this day and constitutes the chief philosophical claim against which liberation theologians struggle intellectually.[5]

This essay reflects what I have been learning even in its preparation: classical christology, as an arena of constructive work, is dead. Its symbolic universe belongs to the history of Christian thought which, when studied honestly, reveals the history of Christian power relations. By that, I mean the history of how the church, in its doctrine, discipline, and worship, has legitimated the use of ecclesial, civil, and social power either to exercise coercive control or to elicit voluntary cooperation.

The first part of the essay is a critical interpretation of the Jesus-of-history and Christ-of-faith postures in christological development. The second part is a preliminary constructive christological effort in the form of notes I used in teaching the christology class.

Beyond "Jesus of History" and "Christ of Faith"

Christology must be redefined as a theological discipline if the Jesus story is to be redemptive for Christian women of different colors, cultures, and classes,[6] for men who are marginalized and kept powerless by those who control the social order often explicitly "in the name of Christ,"[7] and for those who stand as advocates in solidarity with oppressed people and a violated earth. It is this process of redefinition that calls for the re-imaging of Jesus/Christ beyond the traditional dualistic pull between his humanity and divinity—and not only his but ours as well.

Before I began writing this essay I had steered clear of this burial ground of the "God-man" of classical Christian faith by keeping my christological interests under control. I did this by doing what most Christian theologians, however "radical" or "reactionary," "progressive" or "conservative," have done since at least the late patristic period (fifth century C.E.). I refused to "think the unthinkable." I would not think outside the boundaries set by the church fathers as definitive of Christian faith in Jesus/Christ.

As feminist and humanist, I have attempted with others to bring down to earth "high christologies," which tend to prevail in Catholic ecclesiology, and to raise up "low christologies," which often characterize modern Protestantism. From either angle, moving down with divinity or rising up with humanity, I have tried to help produce images of Jesus Christ using terms provided by traditional christology. I have not argued seriously with the classical doctrine that Jesus Christ was and is both divine and human. I still do not. The classical framework has given me both an ideological target for my frustrations with the hierarchical, dualistic foundations of Christian thought and a pastoral and liturgical ground upon which to stand in sharing the language of faith with other Christians. It was in a pastoral spirit of inquiry that I began my work on Jesus of history and Christ of faith.

Leaping into the currents of Christian dualism, I began my christological diving, garbed somewhat awkwardly in gear provided by a coalition of liberation, Anglican, lesbian, and feminist constituencies. Looking for Jesus on the one hand and Christ on the other, I found him—both of him.[8]

I found "Jesus," the man in whom the Logos dwelt, the man whom "enlightened" men have pursued in their quests, old and new, for moral leaders and spiritual friends. I found the brother whose little sister got lost somewhere along the way. I found the fleshly, bloody, suffering, subversive, fully human one from Nazareth.

The term "the historical Jesus" refers both to the discrete historical movement represented by such people as H. S. Reimarus and Friedrich Strauss[9] and to the objective human focus of christology that is done "from below."[10] Since the nineteenth century, the focus on Jesus has represented a rational, humanistic impulse over against the "excesses of supernaturalism."

But the pendulum swing toward Jesus of history is not necessarily an affirmation of humanity. It can serve as a means of perpetuating the notion of a deity who remains above human experience, a god who really is not involved with us. If, in emphasizing Jesus' humanness, we contend that Jesus was "fully and only human" (as I myself wrote a decade ago),[11] such a claim can be interpreted as a rejection of the reality or possibility of incarnation. In any case, to make the historical Jesus one's starting point in christology is to take a reactive posture and, in so doing, to fall in line with the presuppositions of classical christology that divinity and humanity can be comprehended most fully as polar opposites.

Let us move on within the classical framework to the Christ-of-faith perspective, in which the human spirit can be uplifted by faith that God, in fact, became man. In this framework Christ is the Redeemer of Schleiermacher's self-consciousness,[12] the Christ-event of Bultmann's kerygma,[13] and the Spirit of Charity undergirding God's Kingdom in this world according to Frederick Denison Maurice.[14] To know Christ is to worship Jesus as Lord on the basis of a faith that Jesus was and is the Son of God so fully and eternally as to be God the Son. In him we are met, readied, grasped, or otherwise saved from our fallen state.

This Christ is both in and outside time and history. To love the divine savior, who descended from above so that we might ascend in him, is to rise spiritually above the movement of human history. To study this christology is to work "from above." This Christ-of-faith movement has been undergirded by a commitment to the spiritual power of One whose human life was only a partial and momentary occasion in his "larger" life. Such a christology recently has signaled a mystical response to the super-rationalism that in the modern period has taken the forms of naturalism or humanism. In this context, faith in the eternal Christ can (though often it does not) inspire moral courage with which to contend with the principalities and powers of this world on the basis of a higher call to follow Christ rather than the rulers of the present historical order. Such was the faith of some of the nineteenth-century English Tractarians who were wed fiercely to the sacred and eternal relation between the Father and his Christ, the Son, as the locus of salvation.[15]

Bishop Desmond Tutu is a contemporary reminder that adherence to Christ of faith need not lure us away from response to human need.[16] Emphasizing the divinity of Jesus can be a means of sacralizing humanity in the image of Christ. Nonetheless, like the historical Jesus posture, the Christ-of-faith emphasis reflects historically a reactive posture in which we are moved onto the dualistic ground of classical christology in which divinity and humanity are oppositional pulls in our lives and commitments.

Let me move a little further in this critique of the dualistic epistemology of christology as a theological discipline. Writing in 1853 of those searching for "the historical Jesus," Frederick Denison Maurice charged, "Instead of recognizing an impassable chasm between the human and the divine, they became in their minds utterly confounded."[17] He continued, "[The Straussians] conceive Divinity only as an apotheosis of humanity."[18] For Maurice, as later for Barth and other critics of the "Quest of the Historical Jesus," the problem with the intense focus on the human Jesus is that its adherents seem simply to name as "divine" whatever they admire in Jesus, which seems moreover to reflect whatever they admire in themselves. Writing of all such theological attempts to "work up from earthly ground" (foreshadowing contemporary "theologies from below"), Maurice contended that such efforts "form abstractions called 'god,' in which 'God' becomes anything, everything, and nothing."[19]

The warning may be taken by those who look to Jesus to reflect back to us whatever we most admire in ourselves. But is the same temptation not also true for Christ-of-faith theologians? Do such people not also find, mystically "in Christ" rather than rationally in the Jesus story, what they are looking for in their experiences and in their efforts to live "admirably"? Is the "Word of God" of Barth's *Church Dogmatics* necessarily any less self-serving than the "Jesus" of Strauss's *The Life of Jesus Critically Examined?* Is not each of these Christian men, as Schweitzer wrote of Schleiermacher, to some extent in search of the Jesus Christ of his own politic?[20]

The problem in most christological work, whether rooted primarily in Jesus or in Christ, is twofold. First, theologians tend not to acknowledge in what sense they are working for themselves and writing to make sense of their own lives. This is a problem of dishonest praxis. To acknowledge one's self-interest in theological work, far from being "selfish," is to be responsible for what one is authorizing. Second, and the more fundamental problem with the location of christological origins, is the problem named already of a dualistic epistemology. This is a wrong relational way of knowing whatever we know about Jesus, Christ, ourselves, the world, or God.

Wrong Relation in Christological Epistemology: False Knowing

Let me examine briefly the connection between dualism and nonrelationality in christological epistemology. Dualism is steeped in an assumption of opposition: whether in relation to the knowledge of God or Christ, of ourselves or the world, we can know something only insofar as we are *unlike* it. Man is unlike woman. Spirit is unlike flesh. Light is unlike darkness. Heaven is unlike earth. God is unlike humanity. In a dualistic praxis, "the other" is always better or worse, more or less, than oneself or one's people. Identity is forged and known by contrast and competition, not by cooperative relation. Dualism is cultivated in a praxis of alienation between men and women, rich and poor, light and dark, and, in the image of such oppositions, divinity and humanity.[21]

The prevailing shape of Christian anthropology is linked causally and effectively to this problem: in our fallen (sinful) condition, human being is less, and worse, than divine being. In fact, in relation to divinity, we human beings are *bad*. The christological solution to this problem has been historically to assume that, in the person of Jesus, divine and human being overcame the dualism generated by the fall. The split was healed, the brokenness made whole, and now, in the spirit of Jesus, which is Christ, all human beings are called to participate in the ongoingness of this redemptive process.

The problem with this scenario is twofold: In worshiping Jesus as *the* Christ, *the* Son, *the* Savior, we close our eyes to the possibility of actually seeing that the sacred liberating Spirit is *as* incarnate here and now among us as She was in Jesus of Nazareth. We cannot recognize that redemption is an ongoing process which was neither begun nor completed, historically, in the life, death, and resurrection of Jesus. Reflecting this same tendency is the similarly exclusivistic assumption that Christians are *the* people with *the* way, *the* truth, and *the* life. Thus, as Christians, we learn to recognize ourselves primarily as *unlike* "the world," "pagans," "heretics," Jews . . .

Dualism is wrong relation. A dualistic epistemology is steeped in a wrong way of knowing and thus generates false knowledge/lies, about ourselves, others, that which we believe to be divine, and the significance of the Jesus story. Doing christology, as most men have done it, on the basis of wrong relation, is beginning on the assumption that Christians alone are in right relation to God and, as such, have a monopoly on the knowledge and love of God. Another assumption is that it is more important, morally, spiritually, and liturgically, for Christians to preserve a right relation with our own religious heritage than with sisters and brothers who currently inhabit the earth with us. A wrong-relational epistemology, rooted in dualism, causes us to imagine that we know it all—about Jesus/Christ, redemption, God, or ourselves.

Theological narcissism, the preoccupation with oneself and one's god in one's image is a foundational component of the theological structure of ruling class (read here, white affluent Christian male) privilege. This privileged narcissism has been basic to the development of dominant christological models in Europe and the United States in which "God" comes out looking like Charlton Heston and Jesus like Jeffrey Hunter.

We should recognize that this tendency to create divinity in our own image is, to some degree, universal. It is not wrong to create theological and christological images of ourselves. In fact, it is vital to our well-being and to our taking responsibility for what we are doing in the name(s) of God. But more than abstractly wrong, it is destructive of the created/creative world we share to leave the matter there—stuck on one's own "Jesus" or "Christ" image. It is wrong to close the canons at the end of one's own story or that of one's people. This is the epistemological fallacy that has given us the dominant christological image of the blue-eyed, fair-haired Jesus as Lord of all. It is also the twist that provokes Christian objections to the *Christa*, the sculpted image of a full-bodied, nude female Christ on a cross.[22] The universalization of one's own experience has, as its cause, a wrong-relational, dualistic epistemology and, as its consequence, a christology in which the Christian Redeemer with the most salvific power in any situation is the one who comes wrapped in the neatest conceptual package. This christology best serves those who are holding the social, political, and ecclesial power in place.

Both the Jesus-of-history and the Christ-of-faith models of redemption have been constructed historically to combat such narcissism—to challenge, for example, the arrogance of ecclesiastical authorities or the obsessive preoccupation of many Christians with their own interior lives as the beginning and end of "spirituality." But in attempting to correct such mistakes, both Christ-of-faith and historical Jesus images have served primarily to move the debate in a circle, back again into a self-defensive posturing which signals the drawing of christological boundaries around our own sacred icons—be they privatized spirituality or the readily misleading notion that where the bishop is, there is the church.[23]

What has been missing in the dominant structures of Christian faith and discourse has been a *praxis of relational particularity and cooperation.* In this praxis theological knowing would cease to be a matter of discovering *the* Christ and would become instead a matter of generating together images of what is redemptive or liberating in particular situations. In a praxis of relational particularity, we would discover that what is *not* liberating, that is, from a Christian perspective, what is *not* "christic," frequently is that which the Christian churches have associated most closely with Jesus/Christ. What is not liberating is any relationship or system that is closed to discovery, new truths, and self-criticism; unwelcoming of new or "different" people, ideas, possibilities. Creative, liberating interpretations of the Jesus story cannot take root in wrong relation. Such distorted power relations prevent Christians from finding creative and liberating christic meanings in either the Jesus story or their own.

Notes on a Feminist Liberation Christology

Jesus was a Jewish male with a particular relationship to his "abba." "Christ" may be for Christians the salvific implications of the Jesus story. Or "Christ" may be the characterization of justice-making with compassion, courage, and integrity, which can be interpreted as either "human" or "divine" and is, in fact, both at once. *The christological task of Christian feminism is to move the foundations of christology from the ontology of dualistic opposition toward the ethics of justice-making. This happens only in a praxis of relational particularity and cooperation.* Neither the politics, that is, hierarchical power relations, nor the symbolic universe of ruling-class fathers and sons can be a creative, liberating spiritual movement for women, or for poor or otherwise marginalized men. Nor, I think, for any men.

As a feminist theologian of liberation, I have come to believe that an effort to do christology in classical terms (Was Jesus divine? Was he human?) is much like trying to draw fresh milk from a very sick, tired, dry, sacred, and, as it turns out, male goat. Christian feminists and others committed not only to the work of justice but also to holding our theologies and christologies accountable to this work must set new terms for our faith, including, especially, new terms for what we preach and teach about Jesus/Christ and for how we live in relation to the Jesus story and its christic meanings.

Traditionally, christology has been the philosophical study of in what sense Jesus of Nazareth was/is the Christian Messiah or Christ. I offer the following notes as a way into christology from a feminist liberation perspective:

1. Christological truths are rooted in the connections between various particular human experiences, including that of Jesus of Nazareth, in relation to the Sacred: that which gives purpose, value, dignity, and hope to our lives.

2. Christology is an endeavor by Christians to explore the ongoing need for and process of human liberation.

3. While christology is philosophical language about salvation from wrong relation, it is more basically an ethical language of advocacy, love, action, and survival.[24]

4. A basic christological connection we must make is between the

story of the particular man, Jesus of Nazareth, and our stories. This is basic because it is the connection which, historically and communally, has been used and abused as a primary vehicle for organizing the world.

5. Christological truth is neither unchanging nor universally applicable. It is created in the social, historical, personal praxis of right relation, which is always normative, or central, in christology.

6. Christology must be for Christians a collaborative process with roots in confessional, prophetic action shaped by the questions Who are we standing with? and Who are we for?

7. Christology is not a "neutral" process. We do it with, for, and accountable to the poor, women, and all marginalized and trivialized peoples, especially to all who historically have been persecuted "in the name of Christ."

8. Whatever/whoever may be christic for us will emerge in the contemporary crossroads of religious/spiritual pluralism, global movements for liberation from oppression, a feminist commitment to justice for women and to making connections between the liberation of women and of all who suffer injustice, and commitments to a sane and respectful relation to the earth and its varied creatures.

9. Whatever may be christic in the "small places" of our lives is the same spirit of liberation as She who holds the stars and watches over the planets in their courses.

10. Our most fully christic experiences are our most fully embodied (sensual and erotic) connections in relation to one another, other creatures, and the earth.

11. The truths or lies of our christological claims become evident in the fruits of our lives: how we relate to one another and the world.

12. In doing christology, white Christian feminists need to pay especially careful, respectful attention to what Christian feminists and womanists of color are writing and saying about Jesus/Christ, and to what Jewish feminists are writing and saying about anti-Semitism among Christian feminists.

13. Our christologies must be always open to change, ever able to be revised in relation to those whose well-being we do not know or fail to consider, and in relation to the limits of what we are able to know about ourselves or about the Holy in any particular praxis.

2.

Speaking of Christ*

We who are Christians are empowered by the memory and presence of Jesus. The one whom we call Christ mirrors our vocation: to love our neighbors as ourselves and in so doing to offer to God the one spiritual sacrifice God requires of us—to take the risks involved in standing with humankind on behalf of a better world. We look to Jesus as a brother, an advocate, a friend, a liberator, because he stood with us on the earth. Only insofar as we take seriously this human brother can we discern in what he did the divine spirit moving with and in and through him.

In looking at Jesus we see that we are put on the spot to make decisions not unlike his and then to take the consequences. The Jesus story does not let Christians off the hook of our own moral responsibility. Jesus' story is ours not because he lived and died in our stead but because his story mirrors our own lives and spiritual pilgrimages. The Jesus story does not suggest that we do not have to take stands, struggle, suffer, and die. It does suggest that, if we love—stand with— the sacred Spirit that we meet in our sisters and brothers, not public opinion, ecclesial scorn, political repression, or death itself can separate us from this love, which is God.[1]

The life of Jesus is paradigmatic of a human life that is ours as well as his. The Body of Christ is our spiritual identity as a people because the Body of Christ is the physical, tangible, visible network of friends, neighbors, and enemies, options, choices, opportunities, and responsibilities. Through living our daily lives, we are engaged with God. Our communion is holy because together we are empowered to love and

*A longer form of this essay appears as "Can Anglicans Be Feminist Liberation Theologians and Still Be 'Anglican': An Essay on an Improbable Identity" in *The Trial of Faith: Theology and the Church Today*, ed. Peter Eaton (West Sussex, Eng.: Churchman Publishing, 1988). Reprinted with permission.

serve one another, thereby embodying the love of God: our power to form just and compassionate relationships among ourselves.

Sacramentality is a way of seeing one another as bonded, connected organically, members of One Body. It signals our faith in the corporate nature of human life well lived, in the presence of the divine Spirit, which makes us one Body in the actual daily fabric of our lives, in the power of God to act with us, in us, and through us in the ongoing work of creation and liberation. Frederick Denison Maurice, the great nineteenth-century Anglican theologian, teacher, priest, and social activist, was wise in his conviction that whereas it is true that without God we are nothing, it is also true that we are never without God.[2] This means that we are ever able to dip into the infinitely deep wellsprings of justice and act together to shape the realm of God, which even now we may glimpse whenever we notice the fruits of love in our common life.

The focus, albeit controversial, in modern Anglicanism on the incarnational character of the whole creation testifies to how seriously Anglicans may take the profoundly sacramental constitution of our world.[3] Nowhere is this significant emphasis any more apparent than in the contemporary efforts of feminist liberation theologians to offer images of incarnation that do justice to the whole earth and its inhabitants, not merely to the christological preserves of church fathers.[4]

The whole inhabited earth is sacred space in which God lives, breathes, and acts. Sharing this common home, we are One Body. Insofar as we live as such, we reflect the trinitarian character of God as the Lover, the Beloved, and the spirit of Love which binds the Lover to her Beloved. As people created for the purpose of loving one another, all of us are worthy of love—and are responsible for loving. This worthiness and this responsibility, ours by birth, constitutes our holiness and requires that we live in common-wealth, so that all persons and other creatures can live together creatively.

Richard Hooker, a preeminent father of Anglicanism, understood our sacramental heritage as rooted in our "participation" with Christ— "he in us and us in him"—through the liturgy as well as through our general corporate life as the church.[5] The "participation" that Hooker commended provides a useful means of envisioning our moral life and our work together in solidarity with the poor, women, elderly citizens, gaymen and lesbians, members of racial, ethnic, and religious minorities, and all marginalized people. From a feminist liberation perspective, we are able to understand our relationship to Jesus as one of participation. We are *with* Jesus; as such we are *in* Christ.

As participants in the world and church, our lives are literally involved, "rolled up," in one another's—they in us, we in them. We are One Body, a unity, through mutual participation. Whenever any of us is violated, all of us suffer. Genocidal practices waged against Armenians, Jews, Cambodians, Palestinians, Guatemalans, Native Americans, or South Africans assault us all. To struggle for black civil rights in the United States is to act on behalf of the whole people of God. To insist upon women's ordination is to labor in solidarity with all women and men, within and without the church, because right relation in the church "participates" in the larger society's work of justice.[6]

Injustice is the breaking apart of the One Body. Injustice is our alienation from the possibility of living in common-wealth. Injustice is the breeding ground of hatred. It keeps us cut off from one another and from our own spiritual depth. It alienates us from God. Actions or attitudes that disrupt the enjoyment of mutually empowering relations between and among us are sinful. Unjust structures, such as heterosexism, racism, and class elitism, in which our attitudes and actions are shaped, are evil.

Human structures, systems, institutions, and technology are not necessarily ungodly. God's Spirit lives and breathes through us. Together, in our relational matrix, we are God's Body on the earth with one common vocation: to live in right relation. To create mutually empowering relations from which each derives self-respect as well as other survival resources is in fact the substance of love. Where there is no effort to create justice, there is no love. In Christ, we stand with Jesus as we stand with one another and work toward the creation of justice. We love Jesus, as we love one another. In so doing, we love and honor God.[7]

3.

Living for the Living
Theological Lessons from Nicaragua*

"Pray for the dead and fight like hell for the living." With these words, Mother Jones (1830–1930), the Irish-American labor organizer and humanitarian, urged workers not to focus on past deeds, misdeeds, issues, or heroes but to struggle for those exploited today by unjust labor relations. In much this same spirit, Jesus beckoned those with him to "leave the dead to bury their own dead" (Matt. 8:22; Luke 9:60). Recent visits to Nicaragua have cast theologically into bold relief for me what this cryptic challenge may involve—not only for Nicaraguan *campesinas/-os* but for all of us, be we Christians, Jews, Marxists . . . To begin to understand how most Nicaraguans view their struggle is to encounter a way of seeing the world which is foreign to the dominant ethos and values in the United States. Consider the following theological lessons from Nicaragua:

The first lesson is this: *"The living" includes all past, as well as current, inhabitants of planet earth who have been committed to the well-being of humanity.* This is common knowledge in Spanish folk religion, however institutionalized its context may be. Faithful people assume that women, men, and children who have died defending the Nicaraguan revolution against the United States-sponsored *contras* are not dead at all but rather continue to participate in the struggle against *imperialismo*. At the funerals of those killed by *contras*, when the people respond, *"Presente!"* as each name is read, they are not merely asking that those who

*An earlier version of this essay was written in 1986 for *The World: A Journal of the Unitarian Universalist Association*. The purpose of the essay was to reflect on the lessons learned during a trip to Nicaragua. Reprinted with permission.

have died stay with them. They are announcing that those who have died now live. They are proclaiming that those whose bodies are being laid to rest have not gone at all but rather are *presente!*, stronger than ever as a force to be reckoned with, members of a Body that cannot be buried and forgotten. In this sacred spirit, A. C. Sandino, like Jesus of Nazareth and every person who has loved neighbor as self, is alive and well in the ongoing revolutionary struggle for justice: *presente!*

In this same elusive and electrifying spirit, Nicaraguans, Salvadorans, and others who work on behalf of the people are clear that *el pueblo unido jamás será vencido* (the people united will never be defeated)—not even by the giant military-industrial complex which batters down from the north. For most Nicaraguans, as for members of other revolutionary societies and movements, the rulers of the United States are, finally, impotent. With this comes the understanding that a breathing body is not necessarily alive. Just as death cannot separate them from the body, living does not guarantee that we are a part of it. Ronald Reagan may be popular; he is also spiritually dead, as are all who put profit over people and value coercion over cooperation.

Can we hear and share such confidence? Such unabashed faith in the living may bore or puzzle the rational skeptic who does not see beyond the spiral of violence and gross toll in human life which are effected today by the government of the United States. For once, I would echo Karl Barth's charge that "liberals," whether religious or secular, are bound finally to despair, able to put no strong hope in the "affairs of man." I most emphatically do not agree with Barth, however, that the problem is that liberals are too inclined to confuse ourselves with God, or human affairs with those of the divine. To the contrary, I know my faithlessness is found wherever I am not confident enough of the sacred Power in which, along with the rest of creation, we humans are secured. Our problem, our spiritual, social, political, and pastoral problem, is not that we take human life too seriously but that we do not take divine life seriously enough. Thus we fail to discern the presence of the spirit of love, the source of justice, here in our midst—ours to actualize. Our "rational" inability to see that which is invisible to the naked eye is more basically a cultivated incapacity to experience ourselves as involved with the creative, liberative power that moves the struggle for justice in history. Our capacity to make a difference is the ground of our hope.

We in the United States, especially we who are middle-class and white, need to realize that the faith of many Nicaraguans—like that of many black, Latino, Native, and Asian people in the United States (and elsewhere)—is not a product of "religious education." Rather it is the product of having lived among the living rather than the dead, the spiritually dead. It is from the living that we learn to live. From those who are dead spiritually we are taught only how to imitate them, how to linger in this world, perhaps even how to rule it, but

> never to thirst after justice
> never to hunger with the poor
> never to celebrate what we hold in common
> never to live among the living
> never to live!

And so it was that just as I often look to feminist women and men, to lesbians and gaymen who struggle for justice, and to people of color who know that color does still make a difference in these United States, I turned to my Nicaraguan *compañeras/-os*, to teach me lessons in living, to be my spiritual mentors, and to help me touch and embrace the fullness of our Body.

This leads to a second theological lesson I have learned in Nicaragua: *The Body is, first and foremost, human flesh and blood and bones and mouths and tears which require immediate attention.* Traditionally, white Europeans have affirmed "the Body" as a *spiritual* phenomenon, such as "the Body of Christ." In Nicaragua, as is true wherever physical poverty is a major problem, the Body is a physical network. The Body is a visible and tangible challenge for us to embody our moral principles. From the Nicaraguan *comunidades de base cristiana* (Christian base communities) we learn that each human person, every physical body, is valued and empowered as a member of a larger Body. This Body is a community, a neighborhood, a town, and, especially now, in the context of United States aggression, the Body of the nation.

For Nicaragua's revolutionary Christians, the Body of Christ is actively whatever Body—person or group—is struggling against unjust suffering. No one person or group of people, be it nation, religious tradition, race, or gender, has a monopoly on being the Body of Christ. While all who suffer injustice, tragedy, or sickness are in a passive sense the Body of Christ, only those who struggle against the unnecessary suffering inflicted upon others and themselves are participants in actively shaping the sacred story of salvation: the liberation of humanity and of the earth from forces of domination and control. While the Body of Christ is broken in every act of violence, greed, or bigotry, it is rising in every act of solidarity with those who are oppressed, whatever their credo, color, or culture.

Nicaragua's justice-making Christians believe that the physical Body is born, reborn, nurtured, and strengthened in such solidarity. It is that simple. Those who live for the living are the Body that cannot be killed. They are the holiest of sacraments. When we stand together, we are they. This is embodiment, and it is the incarnation of God.

The third lesson that emerges from the Nicaraguan experience is this: *Our responsibility is to live as interdependent members of a Body—which is to be human, fully human.* We are not born into the world to do "better" or to have "more" than others; nor do we come into life to wait out our time here until we can leave again. We are not here merely to take up space, to clutter the world with our possessions and pretensions. We are born into the world to be ourselves—One Body, one creation. We are here to share, to respect one another and ourselves, to work for our common good, to act on behalf of the well-being of all, and, yes, "to pray for the dead and fight like hell for the living." We eat our daily bread, reap our seasonal harvests, teach and learn from one another, invest our income, and enjoy our work and play and prayers together in the sacred knowledge that our lives are connected, deeply bound together, now and forever. Living in this way means being grateful that, at no point in time or space, in things seen or unseen, is any of us actually alone. Together, we are a relational matrix of needs and gifts, demands and supplies, we people and other earth creatures with us.

The spirit that makes us one, the spirit of humanity is, at heart, the spirit of God. Thus our human responsibility is in the beginning and in the end a divine imperative. Most Nicaraguans—Christian and Marxist—assume that this embodied spirit of solidarity has shaped and is sustaining their efforts on behalf of justice for all Nicaraguans. Today as for the past century, this has meant struggling against United States imperialism.

In this spirit, with these *compañeras/-os,* as well as with many feminists in the United States, I count myself a "humanist," a believer in the high value and creative power of human being. As a theologian, I am a grateful beneficiary of the work of such persons as Audre Lorde,

Beverly Harrison, Adrienne Rich, James Luther Adams, and Martin Buber. Broadly speaking, each of these persons, irrespective of religious tradition, is a humanist in that, with much of the human community, she or he calls us to pool our concerted efforts on behalf of human well-being. Yet the contributions of such teachers and writers suggest that the matrices of human life—our justice, our power, our survival re-sources—are far broader, richer, and deeper than those associated popularly with Western humanist tradition. The humanistic basis of our life together is not rooted in the notion of the individual human mind as locus of creative power or in the assumption that belief in the power of human being is *de facto* disbelief in divine power.

Understood as a *radical* commitment to human well-being, human-ism is a sacred posture, a spiritual movement rooted in the experience of our interrelatedness, we people among ourselves and we two-leggeds with the four-leggeds, the wingeds, those whose bellies hug the earth, and the earth itself. The connecting link that draws us toward one another in acts of love and solidarity is the Power that many call God, Holy Spirit, Goddess, Power of Life, Higher Power . . . This Power provides our common ground. She binds us one to another. He calls us to make incarnate and reveal the sisterhood and brotherhood that are our natural and moral birthright.

This interdependent network of humanity, nature, and the Holy One is the spiritual as well as political basis of *Nicaragua libre*. Among the Sandinistas—peasants, health care workers, teachers, and teenagers, as well as sophisticated political organizers—this fundamentally collec-tive, relational image of what it means to be human is assumed to incorporate the best of both Marxist and Christian traditions. It is on this basis that Minister of Culture Ernesto Cardenal is able to say with gratitude that Christianity has helped him become a good Marxist and that Marxism has helped him become a good Christian.

It is this mixture of ideological commitments which most of the political and spiritual leaders in the United States perceive as threaten-ing. For example, both the U.S. State Department and Nicaragua's anti-revolutionary Cardinal Obando y Bravo contend that neither Christianity nor capitalism can be "mixed" satisfactorily with Marxism (or "communism," as Western interests prefer) because "communism" is "atheistic," and "against freedom"—in short, evil. So too are the deeds and thoughts of all who are supportive of or sympathetic to Marxism, be we well-informed, politically sophisticated traitors or naive dupes of the "evil empire."

We come now to a fourth lesson gleaned from the Nicaraguan experience: *It is our responsibility to discern together what is good and what is evil in our own praxis.* Looking beyond ourselves—to authorities "above" us—for this discernment of good and evil renders us powerless to act together for the good because we strip ourselves of our moral agency. Our capacity to know and do what is just, which is the root of our capacity to move with the sacred Spirit, is denied.

To see good and evil through the lens of the Nicaraguan poor, a poverty we in the United States have helped create, we must realize that in the United States today good and evil cannot be discerned for us by our national government and popular media. Those who hold the power over us need to believe that it is good to beat up enemies and, if they are communists, to wipe them out; that it is evil to negotiate or compromise with wicked people (communist, atheist, un-American), and that only weak folks change their minds and admit mistakes. We are told by the keepers of power that nuclear weapons are "peacekeepers" and *corpus christi* (Body of Christ) and that murderers and mercenaries are "freedom-fighters." The leaders of our country historically have implemented policies that have been patronizing and hostile toward the poor. During the Reagan administration, these policies have been explicated and expanded upon unapologetically, even proudly, as destructive of poor and other socially marginalized people as well as of those who struggle for justice at home and abroad.

The President of the United States asks us to swallow a tale of two nations. We are asked to believe that the government of South Africa is essentially benevolent and is doing its best to maintain a decent (i.e., non-communist) social order under difficult circumstances. At the same time we are told that the government of Nicaragua is essentially malevolent and is doing everything it can to destroy socioeconomic values such as "democracy" and "free enterprise" which the United States so admires in places like South Africa, Chile, and Honduras.

In Nicaragua it is not whether something can be labeled Christian or communist which makes it good or evil. It is whether it is liberating, life-affirming, sustaining, and empowering, or whether it is dominating, death-dealing, disrespectful, and destructive.

For citizens of the United States, to do good in the praxis of our nation is actively to oppose our government's foreign policy and much of its domestic policy as well. To do good means to resist, in every concrete way we can, those policies that eschew the principle upon which we claim that United States history, in its finest hours, has been built: the commitment to liberty and justice for all. This is the cornerstone upon which have been founded movements to free slaves, liberate women and children, vindicate the innocent, compensate workers, feed the hungry, and provide sanctuary for refugees. In the current political ethos, which mocks each of these commitments to justice, to do nothing except bemoan our powerlessness, swear at the evening news, and exempt ourselves from blame for what is happening around us is to do evil.

As we learn these four lessons, we will be learning to "pray for the dead and fight like hell for the living." We will be learning to "leave the dead to bury their own dead." And we will be learning to live with and for the living, *presente!* to one another in the Spirit that calls us together to participate in the redemption of the world.

4.

*Crying in the Wilderness**

O God, in our confusion
and suffering, hear us.

From our fear and hatred, Sophia,
save us.

In these times of trouble,
come, Jesus, stand here
beside us.

At times he [Todd] was like a little kid. . . . I'd ask him to sing
me a love song and . . . he'd make up syllables that made no sense
whatsoever and sing them as off-key as his vocal cords would
manage and we would hold each other and laugh as if we would
never let go. . . . I knew it was in fact love songs he serenaded me
with, only he and I were the only persons on earth who understood what he was singing. . . .

There were times when the stress of Todd's illness got the best
of me. But that never lessened my love for him. . . . He went
away too soon. . . . He gave me extraordinary strength and courage. He gave to me love and understanding and compassion.
Because of Todd, everything I do, see, touch has a new meaning. . . . He is in everything around me. . . . I love and miss
[Todd] so much.[1]

Into the lonely fear of such times as these came John preaching in the
wilderness of Judea: " 'Repent, for the realm of heaven is at hand.' For

*Revision of a sermon preached at AIDS Healing Service, Old Cambridge
Baptist Church, Cambridge, Massachusetts, December 1986, and at Cornell
University, Ithaca, New York, March 8, 1987.

this is the one spoken of by the prophet Isaiah, 'The voice of one crying in the wilderness: Prepare the way of the Sovereign, make the paths of the Sovereign straight' " (Matt. 3:2–3).

Is the prophet's cry in vain? Is the waiting to be forever? The wilderness, an infinity? Will those who suffer be sucked into a bottomless pool of unrequited faith, hope, and love?

Or do we actually expect the Holy One to come? And if we expect to be touched by the power of God, what do we expect of ourselves? What must we do to prepare the way for God to come to us, through us, with us, to re-create this world so desperately fraught with disease, despair, oppression, and unjust death?

The Gospel of Matthew gives us a clue: "Repent, for the realm of God is at hand." But, my brothers and sisters, we must be careful of what we choose to repent. Only with the help of the Spirit can we make good sense out of Scripture and understand, in this instance, what we are called to repent. We who currently constitute the Christian church are the temporary authors and guardians of "Christian truth." It is ours to determine and ours to teach. We Christians quite literally must speak for ourselves and we must do so in humble awareness that what we perceive to be true will itself need to be reinterpreted by those whose survival, dignity, or concrete well-being we are failing to notice—or by those to whom we may fail otherwise to do justice. Yet while we must speak the truth humbly, we must not fail to speak it. If we do not take seriously this sacred vocation of Christian interpretation it will be taken from us, as it is in every generation, by false prophets. We must do this, in part, by providing biblical meanings, the substance of biblical narrative and imagery. In so doing, we Christian learners, practitioners, teachers, and preachers are learning together to speak a Word of God, to speak today of "repentance."

Brothers and sisters, AIDS is threatening to create a global wilderness. To date (1986) in the United States alone AIDS has taken the lives of over fifteen thousand men, women, and children. By the most conservative estimates (from the Center for Disease Control), AIDS will kill at least one hundred eighty thousand people in the United States during the next five years. This will be merely a fraction of its global impact, for the AIDS virus is currently wreaking havoc on every continent in the world. In this plague of fear and suffering, we must be clear about what we are called to repent and we must be bold and public in our repentance.

Here in the wilderness of these United States in the late twentieth century, we are called to repent our collusion with the dominant culture of alienation and fear. We are called to repent our complicity in a social ethos in which violence is glorified and tenderness condemned. We are called to repent our support of a religious ethos in which honesty and courage about our lives-in-relation are punished while our "lies, secrets, and silences" (Adrienne Rich) are rewarded. We are called to repent our respect for a glitzy, wealthy culture bred purposely on ignorance and draped contemptuously in flags of false patriotism.

We who are progressive Christians in this reactionary Christian culture need to be well aware of the effects of our complicity, often through our silence, in the face of mounting crisis. We must clearly recognize that AIDS currently serves the interests of those who hold the power in place, such as politicians who make political mileage out of homophobia, the fear of same-gender love. We must be clear that the AIDS culture is the same culture in which money has come to represent special favor through which fewer and fewer people enjoy more and more at the expense of increasing numbers of people who have less and less. Our dominant culture is one of self-righteous terrorism that creates and finances so-called freedom fighters to undermine the only nation in Latin America (except Cuba) with a public, unapologetic commitment to raise up everyone from poverty, disease, and ignorance.

This is our sin, and we are required to repent it if we expect to find comfort in the One who loves justice and seeks mercy, and by those who are transfigured in Her image. What, then, may our repentance involve? And what may constitute our liberation? Who shall heal us? Who shall deliver us from the evil that breaks our Body as a people? How can it be that our divisions shall cease and that every person and living creature shall be at home in the world? How shall it come to pass that the wolf shall dwell with the lamb and the leopard shall lie down with the kid? How shall it be that this suffering world shall be filled with the knowledge of the Holy One who is our justice and our peace?

> O come, O come, Emmanuel,
>   In our confusion and suffering,
>   hear us.

O come, Sophia, come and visit
us with your presence.

O come, Jesus, come, stand here beside us.
In these times of trouble, be present
with us.

Christians and Jews are heirs to an ancient wisdom set forth as
narrative in the Book of Job, a wisdom that suggests that suffering is not
given by God as curse or punishment. The Book of Job also shows that
whether its roots are biological, sociological, mental, or political and
whether we are its victims, perpetrators, or otherwise involved with it,
suffering may become for us an occasion for spiritual action. It is not
that suffering is "good for us"; it is simply that, whatever its causes in
the complex interstices of history, politics, nature, technology, human
sin, human error, human good, and the pathos and grace of God, our
suffering is a mirror of God's own. As such, it can be a window through
which we perceive dimly the compassion of both divinity and humanity. We can find revealed in our suffering the power, passion, and
vulnerability of ourselves as we are created to be—together, interdependent brothers and sisters.

The Fourth Gospel helps map the spiritual ground of our life togther
in the world: "Unless a grain of wheat falls into the earth and dies, it
remains alone; but if it dies, it bears much fruit" (John 12:24). Our
fundamental spiritual problem, exacerbated in an ugly way by the AIDS
crisis, is that we tend to experience ourselves primarily as individuals—
isolated "grains of wheat"—responsible first and often only for ourselves
and our own interests. Through the lens of Johannine theology, this
state of affairs must be viewed as morally bankrupt, theologically false,
and spiritually faithless. It stands in stark opposition to the good news
that in the beginning and in the end God is with us, Emmanuel. We are
assured that this is so because we are with one another, bearers together
of love—God—for one another. Only as our isolation is broken, as the
separate grains "fall into the earth and die," do we begin to live. Thus,
as a people we stand together, and as a people we fall together. As one of
us, or two of us, or fifteen thousand of us, or six million of us, suffers,
so too do we all. This is love, the love of God. It is the root of a
Christian spirituality for suffering, a way of living in the Spirit into
which all who repent are called.

A spirituality for suffering is steeped in solidarity—the voluntary act of standing with those who suffer—offering them no pretense of magical solutions, no theological rationale for suffering, no feigned lightheartedness or denial of pain and fear. A spirituality for suffering which is the way of repentance—whether in relation to people with AIDS, or people with cancer, battered women, or victims of apartheid—involves offering ourselves to one another as we are. In our vulnerability and powerlessness, as well as in the sacred power we are able to generate, we stand together and we fall together.

What then might be an adequate spirituality for helping us cope responsibly with the horror of AIDS? I suggest four elements of such a spirituality:

1. *We must be present.* We must be present to those who are suffering and dying and to those who love them. Knowing ourselves to be no superwomen and supermen, we must find ways together of stepping through the veils of fear, contempt, and bigotry which have hidden us from people with AIDS, from others marginalized in the dominant culture, and from ourselves as we are called to be by a God of love. As we come out into the open we will see the possibility of who we might be in this world: vulnerable, open-minded, spirited bearers of God to one another.

For most of us, to be present to people with AIDS does not, or will not, mean going great distances or stepping far outside our daily routines. Rather it involves being attentive to members of our own families, friends, neighbors, colleagues, classmates, parishioners, students, teachers. We must be present.

2. *We must be prayerful.* Prayer requires a mind open to whatever the Spirit of love may require of us and a heart open to our sisters' and brothers' well-being. Prayer originates in the desire that all shall be well. The efficacy of prayer is seeded in our desire to be among the healers and the healed. We must be willing to be moved by the Spirit of God into helping to create the very conditions for which we pray. We must pray for people with AIDS and for all people that we and they may participate in whatever is required to be healers of this world and to be healed. We must pray.

3. *We must be pastorally responsible.* This means that we must be honest, well-informed, and forthright in response to AIDS. We must learn and speak the truth about AIDS to our families, friends, and colleagues in our homes, schools, churches, and workplaces. We must be clear that while in the United States the large majority of people with AIDS are homosexual and bisexual men, AIDS is not a homosexual disease. It is a monster that devours people throughout the world, a disease that promises not to discriminate on the basis of sexual preference, gender, race, or spirituality. We must learn the truth and speak up and out to those who need to hear voices of reason and compassion in this season of madness and contempt. We must be pastorally responsible.

4. *We must be politically active.* This means that we must contend against social attitudes that classify and limit—homophobia, sex-phobia, misogyny, racism, and class injustice. These attitudes contribute to the AIDS epidemic here by impeding attempts to educate children about sex or drugs. They impede judicious attempts to keep AIDS from spreading without jeopardizing the dignity, well-being, and lives of those who have AIDS. They impede efforts to understand AIDS as our common problem rather than as something happening largely to hapless individuals.

As long as AIDS is with us, we must protect people with AIDS from our society. We must also protect people with AIDS, and others as well, from the church's twisted demands that we deny the sacred character of our bodies, our sexualities, and our pleasure. We must protect ourselves and others, people with and without AIDS, from Christian teachings that require that we be ashamed of rather than delighted by our deeply erotic and spiritual sensibilities as sisters and brothers on the earth, embodied images of a God of love and flesh. A spirituality of suffering, the active means of our repentance, requires that we Christians be politically active.

The cry in the wilderness, the voice of the prophet in this season of repentance, is an invitation to participate in the passion of that which is most fully human and fully divine. For Christians it is an invitation to participate in Christ: Ours is a Body, given for all. Ours is Blood, shed for all. In our living and in our dying, with AIDS and without AIDS, before and after the cure for which we pray is found, our spiritualities shall be steeped in the connections we discover with one another, as we learn more and more how to live together, members of One Body.

With one another, those here now and those gone on to another dimension of sacred time/space, we are moving a little more into the realm in which

> the captives are made free,
> the blind see,
> the lame walk,
> and the oppressed are set at liberty.

5.

*The "Not Yet" of Women's Rights**

Today, the second Sunday in Advent, is Human Rights Sunday, when we join other Christians worldwide in pledging our commitment to do what we can in solidarity with those whose rights are violated or denied altogether. In particular, we turn our attention today to the rights of women, rights that remain unrealized throughout the world.

As most women in the world become poorer and less in control of their lives today than they were twenty years ago,[1] the goal of women's rights continues to be trivialized, often by good men and women who insist that women's issues and related matters of sexual liberation be relegated to the bottom of serious justice-making agendas.

The United Nations, ever compelling in its idealism, did not come close to grasping the radical character of women's oppression in either its 1949 "Universal Declaration of Human Rights" or later documents such as its 1967 "Declaration on Elimination of Discrimination Against Women." In the former, women's rights are mentioned only in the context of securing women's position in the patriarchal family as wife and mother. The 1967 document, which focused explicitly on the rights of women, fails to convey serious recognition of the massive social and economic upheavals that would accompany the realization of women's rights anywhere on earth. It reads like a fantasy, so little resemblance does it bear to most women's actual life-experiences. Still, in this document, set forth almost twenty years ago, the United Nations signaled a modest vision of what the world *ought* to be, in particular, what the relation of women and men *ought* to be and is *not yet*.

The seasons of the church year reflect our redemptive journeying as a

*Based on a sermon guideline prepared for a publication of the Human Rights Office, National Council of the Churches of Christ, as part of the observance of Human Rights Week 1986. Material used with permission.

people gathered together and as individuals. They help us understand the rhythm of our movements for liberation. Advent is the season in which we name and celebrate that which is "not yet"—goals such as the liberation of women, which we may have heard about or even have known but which have not been fully realized among us, between us— or within us.

There are at least three questions we can ask ourselves during the season of the "not yet," this protracted period of frustration for many women, of confusion for all of us, and, worst of all, of violence that is legislated and adjudicated against poor and marginalized people, mostly women and children, throughout the world.[2] We cannot merely ponder these questions for a few moments, sit down and write out answers, then stand on street corners and hand the answers out to all who pass by. They are questions of conscience-commitment, and we must use them to guide our actions as we move through life. Both women and men must wrestle with such questions. The first question, though, must be put to women, the second to men. The third is universal.

1. *What shall women do on behalf of our own liberation?* To wait passively for others to "give" us our rights to justice, work, bodily integrity, and ordination, to name but a few, is to wait forever. It is, moreover, to wait without faith and to linger in the despair, depression, or indifference that accompany feelings of powerlessness. The Christian message is one of empowerment. For women, the Christian message is a feminist challenge to take ourselves seriously as subjects of our own lives. To be people of God is to be able to act together on behalf of the whole creation which groans in travail.

2. *What shall men do in solidarity with women's liberation?* Men of all colors, classes, and cultures need to be aware that sexism cuts across these many lines that divide men from men and often becomes, reprehensibly, that which unites man with man. Roman Catholic and Protestant men run the risk, for example, of constructing ecumenical "unity" on the basis of the subjugation of women under male authority, all in the name of a "Father" God and "his Son." For men, the Christian message is also a feminist call to stand with women who are struggling to be the subjects of our lives, co-creative agents of our liberation.

3. *How shall we men and women sustain a "revolutionary patience" (Dorothee Soelle) and be serene lovers of the real world in which we live today?* Can we

live even now in the peaceable realm that the prophet Isaiah describes as one in which wolf and lamb dwell together, as do the calf and the lion and the fatling? Can we be a gentle people, wise and angry enough to love well in a world in which frightened people turn vicious and do despicable things? May we pray for deliverance from the temptation to participate in such violence and for the courage to stand publicly against the doings of violence.

The realm of God, in which serenity is rooted, is a way of being in relation to one another in which we are resources of the Spirit for one another. To honor and respect one another is to know and love God. It is a way of sharing and discovery, rather than of ownership and control. It is a way of common wisdom and common people, rather than of superstars, saviors, and eternal truths. We move along this common way toward the future rather than being stuck in the past, for it will not do to boast that we have Abraham as our father, Jesus as our Lord, Mary as our Lady, or God on our side. In God's realm, we are known by the fruits of our lives, not by our ancestors' lives or our religious principles.

In this season of the "not yet," we wait for the birth of Christ. May we learn more deeply from the Jesus story that "Christ"—the cooperative relation between divine spirit and human being—is born in every moment of our commitment to love and justice on the earth. God has acted and acts now. So we are told by those who have left us a legacy of faith—Moses, Miriam, Hagar, Mary, Jesus, Paul, Martin Luther King, Jr., Archbishop Oscar Romero, Chief Albert Luthuli, Victoria Mxenge, Isaac Muofhe.[3] Our question is not when or how *God* will act to save women, men, and the earth itself, but rather when and how *we* will act.

6.

Daring to Discern Divinity
A Homily Before Theological Examinations*

The Twelfth Day of Christmas comes, with its brittle fir trees in garbage heaps, reminding us of people, places, love, loneliness, what has been gained and lost, and whatever else has touched us in these recent days gone by. This same eve of the Epiphany brings us to a moment of anticipation in which we stand in that almost-but-not-yet posture, reaching for some revelation of the purpose and meaning of what "it" is all about, these people and places, loves and losses, celebrations and grief, our lives, and our work. What are we doing? From a liturgical perspective, it is too soon to say, so we wait . . . for a star, a sign, an assurance that we are headed in the right direction.

But our lives do not run on a liturgical clock. In less than an hour, some of you will begin your General Ordination Examinations (GOES).[1] You will be put on the spot to say something about what it all means and to give evidence, as it were, that you have seen the same star that led those wise ones once upon a time toward a new experience of the purpose, activity, and presence of a God who is with us.

What the GOES and any theological examination should be testing is the strength of our purpose in the world/church as persons who have experienced God. We do not know yet whether or not the exam this year has been designed to elicit information reflecting the personal integrity and intellectual staples of vocational purpose. The point is, it should. It is, of course, a challenge for anyone being tested to put this examination to constructive use and to allow the strength of vocational

*Revision of a sermon preached at the Episcopal Divinity School, Cambridge, Massachusetts, January 5, 1984.

purpose, with the intellectual facility that supports it, to come through. As always, to do this involves some risk if one's purpose and commitment is creative and formidable.

Let me speak briefly to the cooperation of human and divine purpose. In November 1983, along with a dozen other women from the United States, I visited about 150 members of a Christian base community in the agrarian community of Esteli, Nicaragua. In this community, we heard laypeople, priests, children, women, and men—all of them Christian revolutionaries—bear witness to a clear, unequivocal faith in the purpose and plan of a God whom they have come to know through each other. In meeting one another as human beings with real and particular needs, dreams, lives, and goals, they have come into relationship with divine life, activities, and purpose. This was their witness to us, their understanding of a gospel which has as much to do with our lives here as with those of revolutionary Christians in Nicaragua.

We heard this morning in Isaiah 61 a statement of the prophet's certainty in God's purpose. The passage brings to a close chapter 61, in which God's purpose is spelled out: justice, righteousness, right relation. Of God's desire and capacity to effect justice in the world, Isaiah has no doubt. "As the earth brings forth its shoots, and as a garden causes what is sown in it to spring up, so the Sovereign God will cause righteousness and praise to spring forth" (Isa. 61:11). This single-willed purpose of God is not only right, it is natural and simply the way it is.

But how is this purpose made real and effective among us? It is right, it is natural, but it does not "just happen" any more than any good relationship or well-informed ministry "just happens."

The Fourth Gospel suggests that the Word, or Logos, is God's purpose and our own, as persons created through the purpose and in the image of God. Divine purpose, which we are created to reflect and live as our own, creates life where death reigns and hope where despair runs rampant. Divine purpose grounds our common well-being and commands our allegiance to one another.

The root-source of our vocational purpose as Christians is to create life in the midst of death and despair. It is to move swiftly on behalf of right relation in our world and church. It is to accept the fact that by the Spirit this creative activity, the purpose of all divine life, is ours to embody as sisters and brothers of Jesus. Christians call him "Christ" because Jesus was one in whose life the unity of purpose between God and humankind became evident. Each time we speak of "Christ," we are saying something about ourselves, about all women and men and our capacity to act in unity with the purpose of God. This critical faith in ourselves as persons called to act in unity of purpose with God is the foundation of everything worthwhile in the world. Certainly every theological examination of Christian ministers should be designed to elicit critical reflection upon the intellectual framework of such faith.

As you work on your exams, do not forget the point of it all: Our purpose, by God's grace, is to act on behalf of human well-being. We are to bring life where there is disease, oppression, pain, and despair. We are to live in the assurance that God is indeed incarnate: She is here, He is here, insofar as *we* are here to act in concert with this most gracious of Spirits. In this faith, you can rest assured that no test in the world, finally or for long, can dampen your spirit, break your commitments, or erase the glimmers of your hope or humor.

7.

*Learning to See**

Epiphany is not merely a season of "showing forth," in which the meaning of Jesus is made manifest to those who seek him. The Epiphany of God's power, God's love, and God's justice on the earth, in order to mean anything at all, requires that we see what in fact is revealed in Jesus. The Epiphany requires that we learn to see what is already happening around us, between us, and within us in this world. The Epiphany invites us to see what God is doing in the world and to understand what our lives, commitments, and work may involve if we take seriously our vocation as people of God.

As we learn to see more clearly through the eyes of God, we will catch a glimpse of the star of Bethlehem and see not only who lay in that manger two thousand years ago but who lies there, still cast out of respectable inns and eating places; still relegated to the margins of our religious institutions, society, and nation; still the brunt of racist, sexist, anti-semitic, homophobic, cruel, and demeaning jokes; still the object of fear, scorn, and contempt; still bound to be crucified. Still today we crucify the daughters and sons of God, our sisters and brothers on this earth, because still today we liberal Christians fail more often than not to see what is actually happening. Without this ability to see we will find ourselves also unable to believe—unable to believe not only in a God of justice and compassion, but also in ourselves as her friends, compañeras, and helpmates.

O God, may we believe, with the psalmist, that we shall see your goodness in the land of the living. May we be strong. May our hearts take courage. For these are not easy days.

*Revision of a sermon preached at Christ Church, Cambridge, Massachusetts, on February 8, 1987.

How then shall we learn to see sacredly so that we might believe? First, we must learn to look in unexpected places for the love and grace and power of God. Habakkuk, in keeping with the rest of the prophetic tradition of Israel, warns that even as God's glory covers the heavens, even as the earth is full of God's praises, even as the "brightness" of the divine—the splendor of the very power of love itself—"flashes" among us, God will be veiling God's power.

Now what is this all about? It is about the fact that God seldom takes the shape we expect. God rarely conforms to our expectations of what a God of power and might "should" look like. We are to look for God in the places we do not expect to find power or might on the earth, among the least of these, our brothers, sisters, and other earth creatures. There, and there only perhaps, are we likely to be encountered by the Holy One of Israel, whom Jesus called *abba* (daddy), and who, in truth, is also the mother of us all, the source of our birth, the wellspring of love in history, the root of all justice—and compassion. God is always veiled, hid from full view. She is perceptible only to eyes of faith. For only eyes of faith are able to see what Paul calls the "secret and hidden wisdom of God" (1 Cor. 2:7)—the fact that the Divine Presence seldom has much to do with the "good order" of religion and society. She has, however, everything to do with the inclusion of those whom the custodians of good order have cast out because they are the wrong color, culture, creed, class, because they have the wrong nationality or wrong sexuality, or because they have the wrong ideas or the wrong questions. As Paul noted in his letter to the people of Corinth, "Not one of the rulers of this age understood that; for if they had, they would not have crucified the Sovereign of glory" (1 Cor. 2:8).

Still today, if the rulers of this nation understood this secret, they would not be killing the peasants of Nicaragua, the miners of South Africa, or the poor and destitute of our own land. If we understood that God's presence is hidden in this world among the least of our brothers and sisters, and in the places of our own lives that seem to us least important, we would not compute our worth by measuring our successes in relation to those who hold authority in the various institutions of our common life. To the extent that we *are* those in authority, we would understand that our relation to God depends upon our willingness to risk losing this authority, this institutional power and privilege. Such risk is necessary if we are to be faithful to the One who lives and moves most closely and intimately with those who are poor, marginalized, and outcast in relation to our society and, too often, our churches.

So, we must look first in unexpected places if we are to see God's epiphany—in places like mangers, prisons, AIDS wards; most often in places other than church and in religions other than Christianity. We must look even in the most unlikely places of our lives, in our own shabby, secretive, scary closets.

The second lesson that we must learn in order to see sacredly is courage: to see beyond the fear that impedes our capacity to know or love God.

Let me tell you a story. Some time ago, along with twelve other theologians from the United States, I attended a ten-day seminar in Cuba, hosted by Cuban Episcopalian, Presbyterian, and Methodist theologians. Having grown up with a fear of communist Cuba, a fear that is as "American" as the flag, I was at first shocked to learn that there are churches and theologians in Cuba. Who would guess it from listening to the propaganda of our "free press"? While in Cuba, I attended several Episcopal churches and was invited to preach and preside at a Eucharist in the cathedral in Havana. After the service, an old, bent-over woman approached me with a broad smile and outstretched arms. In her Spanish and my "Spanglish" we managed to communicate. She was ninety-one years old, and the only member of her family who had remained in Cuba after the 1959 revolution. "Now, my young priest and sister," she said, her eyes sparkling, "it is such a blessing to meet a person from the United States who is willing to see for herself what we have done. Now, I'm not a communist, I'm a Christian—a life-long Episcopalian. But I want you to know that twenty-five years ago children lay dying out there on the street, sick and starving; women lay in brothels, exploited and abused; most people in Cuba could not read or write. Those were cruel and vicious times and the United States supported this cruelty and oppression. Today, in Cuba, this communist nation of ours, there are no children starving in the streets and fewer women are exploited and abused anywhere—in brothels, family, or business. Nearly everyone in Cuba today can read and write. Poverty has been eliminated, and this country has become miraculously a model of what can happen when wealth and power are shared. I believe that Cuba is a light to the nations. And now I ask you, one Christian to another, is this not the will of God? Is this not what Jesus would have us do? To feed the hungry, liberate the oppressed, offer hope to the exploited? Is this not the work of Jesus?"

Unless we can see through our well-learned fear, we are unable to hear the gospel in this wise old woman's words, or in the words of John Diamond, an Afro-American theologian in our delegation who preached in a Presbyterian church in Cuba. In his sermon, Dr. Diamond spoke of how terrified he had been of coming to Cuba. In fact, he would not have come if his seminary president had not insisted. He was terrified of "communism," "Marxist-Leninism," "Cuba." He had expected to be followed, bugged, and wired everywhere he went. Then he explained that he had found that, after living for six decades as a black person in the United States, his week in Cuba was the first time in his life that he had ever felt entirely free of the colorline—as if, in Cuba, his being black really did not make any difference. To have had this experience at least once in his lifetime left him deeply grateful.

Through the eyes of fear, we see only those "gods" set before us by the rulers of our time. We cannot perceive the work of the Spirit that animated Jesus as long as we are blinded spiritually by the fear that makes us angry at beggars in the street rather than about an economic order that generates poverty and greed. We must learn to see courageously beyond the fear that impedes our efforts to know and do the will of God.

This brings us to the third lesson we need to understand in order to see through the eyes of the sacred: we Christians in the United States must learn to discern more carefully the fabric of creation, the tapestry of liberation, and the designs of God's blessing than we have learned as citizens of this well-intentioned but badly misguided nation that most of us love. The United States is, for most of us, home, and for many of us, a good home. But, my friends, that is not enough. We who are Christians in the United States must learn to see beyond the libertarian . . . the "I did it my way, it worked for me" brand of civil religion which currently is so much in vogue and which has its twisted roots in a badly mistaken doctrine of "freedom."

You may have seen the marvelous Public Broadcasting System series on the United States civil rights movement, *Eyes on the Prize*. Episode 3, "Ain't Scared of Your Jails (1960–61)," concentrated on the first sit-ins in Nashville, Tennessee, in 1960. There was an interview with a white

woman who said, "I think that people who strive to gain social accept-
ance through . . . [what] they call nonviolent or passive resistance . . .
are the most violent. I also think that it is in violation to my civil rights
if someone can say 'You must serve me.' . . . [I]f a man owns an eating
establishment, if he can't choose whom he pleases to serve, or not to
serve, that can affect me, and you, and anyone else."[1]

This declaration should not be heard as an anomaly, one strange
statement in isolation, by one racist Southern woman. The woman was
mouthing a mistaken, immoral, and commonplace tenet of United
States society: Every person—particularly every white, ostensibly heterosexual, affluent male—has a fundamental right to do whatever he
wants to do with *his* property, *his* family, *his* life, *his* nation, and he has
no equally fundamental responsibility to act on behalf of the well-being
of others. In this context of racial and sexual entitlement, to legislate
justice for blacks, for women, for gaymen and lesbians, for the poor, for
Spanish-speaking citizens, for the sick, for anyone, does indeed in-
fringe upon *his* "freedom."

Christians in the United States (especially we who are Anglo and
others who have acquired some access to economic or social power)
often fail to see that our fundamental identity is not as individuals with
"rights" but as members of One Body, interdependent and mutually
responsible for one another. This is not simply a spiritual truth. It is
literally true that as long as anyone is a slave, in bondage, cast out,
marginalized, trivialized, we are all of us diminished, broken people.

Theoretically, Episcopalians should know this. We have a great theology of "participation," community, and shared responsibility. Think
of John Donne's "No man is an island," and of the lives and work of
such Anglicans as William Temple, Pauli Murray, and Desmond Tutu.
Too often, however, our vision falls short and we fail to see through the
sham of the brouhaha and false patriotism on behalf of the "freedom" of
every man to do pretty much as he pleases. As the old saying goes,
"Here's to you and here's to me, in hopes that we don't disagree. But if
in case we disagree, to hell with you and here's to me." Upon this
irresponsible credo stands the popularity of our current president,
Ronald Reagan. We must learn to see through the fallacy of this
perverted notion of freedom if we hope to see and recognize the faces of
God around us and among us.

The fourth and final lesson that we need to comprehend to see sacredly is offered by the Gospel of Matthew, in which we are told something about what we must learn to see in ourselves: we are empowered to act by the force of love itself, embodied among us, God incarnate.

If we spend our energies searching the "heavens" and "spiritual things," trying to rise above the clutter of our daily lives, we will not find the God whom Jesus loved. We must learn to see that to be the salt of the earth, flavorful and tasty; to be the light of the world, not hidden but rather illuminating God's presence in the world, is to be epiphanies ourselves. We are called in this season to be bright manifestations of the power of God in history. Our vocation is to join Jesus and many others in giving God a voice, giving God an embodied life on earth. By the power of the Spirit which we witness in the life, death, and resurrection of Jesus, to be the salt of the earth and the light of the world is to be "in Christ," the active cooperative movement between divine and human being on this earth. As we learn to see sacredly we will know where we are called to be and what we are called to do. We will find ourselves able to believe in both God and ourselves as empowering friends, *compañeras/-os*, and helpmates.

8.

*The Spark Is God**

If we burn with a passion for human well-being, the spark is God. One of the most theologically complex affirmations made by Christians is that it is not we ourselves but the Spirit who brings life, does good, bestows love and grace and justice upon the world. Then again, one of the most morally complex affirmations made by Christians is that we must assume responsibility for what we do. It is indeed we ourselves who bring life or death, we who do good or evil, we who bear grace and justice in the world or who cast shadows of fear and denial as we slip through the time we are given and call it life.

The tension between affirming ourselves as God-bearers and confessing that we ourselves do nothing except serve as receptive channels for a god who initiates all that is good constitutes a basic experiential and doctrinal strain in Christian life and history. Most of the major historical disputes in the church, the Arian and Pelagian controversies, for example, have origins in this tension: *I, yet not I*, am responsible for whatever good *I, yet not I*, have done. The dynamic tension is critical and it is here to stay, not to be resolved. But understanding its dynamic may help a bit in experiencing its redemptive character.

In Acts 14, we read about Paul and Barnabas, who are zealous in preaching and healing in the name of Christ. Because these Christians are effective ministers—the crippled man actually walks—Paul and Barnabas are mistakenly identified as Hermes and Zeus, that is, as gods, not human beings. From the perspective of disbelieving witnesses, an act of God cannot be accomplished by a human being. For the Christian to be actually effective as a healer, teacher, prophet, preacher, he or she must be "more than human," for only gods can

*Revision of a sermon preached at the Episcopal Divinity School in 1984.

manifest such power. Such a person is at best a vehicle by which God acts. Here, in the dualistic assumption that we are nothing unless God, at God's own initiative, uses us, is where much Christian doctrine has gotten stuck. The problem from a moral perspective, and it is a moral issue of enormous proportion, is that it renders us irresponsible as spiritual, moral agents.

To assume, with the early, disbelieving onlookers, that if it is really good it must be a god and not a human being is to perpetuate false assumptions about both deity and humanity. Human being, human flesh, human desire, and human choice are not, by nature, ungodly or anti-God. Divinity does not "naturally" move in opposition to human need, human discovery, and human passion. The life of the Creator is intimately bound up with the creation, so much so that without God, we are nothing. And, without us, for all practical, daily purposes in this world, God, the power of love in history, is dead.

How can we understand the cross and the resurrection other than as a sign that all is not in vain when one loves God with the passion of a Jesus? And how do we understand the gas chamber in Auschwitz or death squads in El Salvador? Wherever we abdicate our responsibility to pick up our beds and walk, refuse our vocation to act on behalf of sisters and brothers who need advocacy, we damage one another with no less deadly consequence than the act of the Roman state against Jesus.

God has spoken already and speaks constantly. God calls us in the ongoing process of creation itself. We are born to be lovers. To wait for God to tell us how to live, much less to live for us without affecting us much one way or the other, is to live no good life at all. If we are not authorized *already* to see God in the faces of our friends and enemies, people known and unknown to us, and if we have not heard *already* the voices of God in daily news reports, classrooms, chapel, homes, parishes, and workplaces, we wait in vain for God to call. For even if She should rise from the dead, we would not believe!

In John 14, Jesus responds to the question of how he will manifest himself to his disciples once he is gone. "If any love me, they will keep my word, and God my Father and Mother will love them, and we will come to them and make our home with them" (John 14:23). Love is an action, the act of respecting deeply all created beings and of acting on behalf of the well-being of those whom we love. The first word in Jesus' statement is extremely important: *if*. *If* we love, God comes and makes a home with us. God's life with us is contingent upon our love, our opening our lives, lifting up our hearts, saying what we must, doing what we can, sharing what we are and have. This is a far cry from the image of our human flesh as an empty vessel, a passive receptacle, which on its own initiative can do nothing. The point is, God has taken the initiative, and God's initiative is our birthright. Thus, Jesus' friends, like Jesus himself, are to assume a capacity to speak and act for the good, which is for God. Insofar as we do so, God comes to us and comforts us.

What then distinguishes this moral theological affirmation from the "work-ethic," the doctrine of salvation by works, which has reflected the mistaken notion that our redemption can be earned by an accumulation of credits, accomplishments, hard work, and good deeds? The clue to the difference is in Jesus' words of assurance to his disciples after he has told them that they must love him if they are to be visited by God. "These things I have spoken to you while I am still with you. But the Counselor, the Holy Spirit whom God will send . . . will teach you all things, and bring to your remembrance all that I have said to you" (John 14:25–26).

What enables us to do anything that is loving or just? It is the knowledge that we will experience in our lives what Jesus experienced in his—the Holy Spirit sent by God to counsel, comfort, and teach us. It is this Holy Spirit that reminds us of what is *already* ours to know: we are commissioned not by special privilege nor by being set apart, but because we are human beings, born into the world, members of the human family. We are called to love one another.

Without love, we are nothing. Without love, we are nothing but empty vessels, clashing cymbals, passive receivers, brittle shells of human being. Lots of running around, doing things, accumulating achievements will lead us nowhere. By the Spirit we are called to love. Insofar as we love, our lives are inspired. And God finds a resting place with us.

Insofar as we are lovers of human and created life, bearers of compassion and courage, justice-makers, visionaries, and workers for a better world, *it is we ourselves who do these things by the power of the One Spirit who has called us to this life together.*

In this same Spirit and in the terribly urgent time of human need in which we live, may we hear well the implicit call of Nikos Kazantzakis:

> The ultimate most holy form of theory is action. Not to look on passively while the spark leaps from generation to generation, but to leap and burn with it. [1]

It is in our cooperation with a God who is love and who acts in history through us, that we may find the peace that the Spirit, in Her Wisdom, has made available to us from the beginning.

9.

*Humility**

Dear sisters and brothers, my thanks to Bishop Hernandez,[1] and to all of you, for this opportunity to be with you today as we worship our Creator and Liberator. I bring with me warm greetings from many men and women in the United States who are joined with us here today. They are with us in the Spirit of the Holy One who labors by day and by night throughout the entire world to bring justice and peace, compassion and comfort, to persons of all countries, cultures, races, and religions.

The lessons we have just read from the Bible teach us about what is involved in living as faithful people of God. Each lesson contains a different yet related message. The first message that I hear in today's readings is that we are to be humble. In the Epistle of 1 Peter, we are told that God resists the proud and gives grace to the humble. "Humble yourselves therefore under the mighty hand of God" (1 Pet. 5:6a). What might this mean for us—whether we are Cubans or United States citizens? Humility does not mean that we are supposed to walk around with holy faces and pious expressions, trying to look as if we do not care for ourselves or anything else except a "god" who lives above us in the heavens. Humility does not mean that we are insignificant or tiny or worthless creatures under the hand of an almighty God or in comparison to other people who are more important than we ourselves. No, my friends, humility is a sign of our common humanity. It means that we hold all things that matter to God in common. In the eyes of God,

*Revision of an English translation of a sermon preached in the Episcopal Cathedral, Havana, Cuba, June 23, 1985. The Reverend Dr. Adolfo Ham was enormously generous in offering to translate this sermon from English into Spanish.

we all are precious, glorious earth-creatures who matter a great deal to God and should matter deeply to ourselves and one another.

To affirm and care for ourselves is not what the Bible means by pride. To ask for what we need to survive, to live with dignity, and to be treated with respect and compassion—this is not pride! When we hear that "God opposes the proud but gives grace to the humble" (1 Pet. 5:5c), we are hearing that God acts against those who believe themselves to be better than others and to deserve special privileges and special rights in this world. To be proud is to be puffed up with the assumption that our lives are worth more than the lives of other people, that our way is best, and that no one else is as good, or as important, as we are. This is the pride that God despises and rejects and that separates us from God.

So, to be humble means that we realize that our place is alongside everyone else in the world. It is to expect no special privilege or treatment for oneself, one's people, or one's nation, but rather to expect to give and receive in the same measure as others. To be humble means to know ourselves as no more or less valuable than anyone else in the world. A humble man or woman knows that he or she exists in relation to all others and is brother or sister to the rest of creation. She or he knows that this commonality and relativity are good. It is in fact our holy ground, in which the purpose and will of God is rooted.

The second message I hear in today's readings is from the passage in Luke (15:4–10). God does everything possible to seek us out when we are overcome by our pride. No stone is left unturned, no human heart unattended, in God's efforts to try to convert us to humility. If there is one proud, arrogant, haughty person, God will search high and low for ways of bringing this person to humility. If there is one proud, arrogant haughty nation, God will do everything God can do to touch the heart of this nation so as to make it humble. Even today, God is searching high and low to touch the heart of the United States because my country, which I love, has become puffed up with pride.

Just as the shepherd leaves the ninety-nine sheep in order to find the one who is lost and the woman sweeps her house in search of one lost coin, the God who is our Father and Mother searches day and night to try to rescue those people and nations who have been lost as they puffed up with an arrogant, destructive sense of being better than everyone else.

And please hear what a compassionate God we have! God seeks out the proud to convert, not to judge. God does not seek to condemn the proud, but rather to save. For God knows that proud, arrogant people and nations are not happy people, but are desperate and frightened folks who are damaging not only other people but themselves as well.

The third and less explicit message I hear in today's readings from Scripture is a message basic to our lives as people of God. It is about the power of grace. "God . . . gives grace to the humble" (1 Pet. 5:5c). This means, I believe, that through a particular gift—grace—God gives humble men and women the power and strength to embody God among us here on earth. People who know they are related to one another and who share their common resources help make God incarnate in the world. Without humility it is not possible for God's grace to move in our lives, and to make God real and tangible in our lives and the lives of others.

We witness in the life of Jesus the power of God's grace at work among Jesus and his friends. We say that we believe that God was in Jesus. Whenever we call Jesus "Christ," we are saying that we believe that, through the life of the very humble Jesus, God's grace was especially powerful. My sisters and brothers, we—no less than Jesus—are called by God to live humble lives and in so doing to help bring God's power again and again into the midst of human affairs. We are called to be humble and in so being to be the Body of Christ, fully alive with a Spirit both human and divine. This means literally that our hands are God's hands in the world and our bodies, the Body of Christ. Transubstantiation indeed!

In closing I want to tell a story. It is about a man who, in the early nineteenth century, was the captain of a ship that transported Africans in chains to the United States to work as slaves. This captain, John Newton, was a proud Englishman—arrogant, unjust and puffed-up with a belief that he and other white people were superior to Africans. While serving on this ship he became a Christian. Now, naming himself a Christian was not enough. He continued to work on the ship for another six years. I believe that through all of this time God was searching for him and seeking a way to show him humility. When he did leave the ship it was because his health had begun to fail. At that time, 1754, he wrote, "The slave trade . . . is indeed a genteel employment and is usually very profitable, though to me it did not prove so, the Lord, seeing that a large increase in wealth would not be good for me."[2] Yet God kept looking for him, trying to find a way to teach him humility.

After he left the slave trade, Newton studied and became a priest. After many years, he finally began to speak out against slavery and the slave trade, writing in 1788, "I hope it will always be a subject of humiliating reflection to me, that I was once an active instrument in a business at which my heart now shudders."[3] As priest to William Wilberforce, a member of Parliment, he was influential in Wilberforce's forty-four-year leadership in the drive to abolish slavery in England.

Somehow God had touched Newton's heart and humbled him. We know this because he wrote a hymn about what he had experienced. It is a hymn the words to which many of us know. Few of us, however, know its history.[4] I will close with it.

> Amazing grace, how sweet the sound
> That saved a wretch like me
> I once was lost, but now am found
> Was blind, but now I see.
>
> 'Twas grace that taught my heart to fear,
> And grace my fears relieved;
> How precious did that grace appear,
> The hour I first believed!
>
> Through many dangers, toils, and snares
> I have already come
> 'Twas grace that brought me safe this far
> And grace will lead me home.[5]

10.

*For All the Saints**

Michelle Peña Herrarra
Nalvia Rosa Meña Alvarado
Cecilia Castro Salvadores
Ida Amelia Almarza

Hay una mujer desaparecida . . . en Chile . . . [1]

I invite you to remember with me the saints. The church is founded on the act of remembering. We remember the Jesus story, and we remember the rest of the Christian story still in the making. We are makers of Christian history. Our capacity to make this history a story of love, compassion, and justice is rooted in our capacity and willingness to remember those past and present whose lives touch ours and have in some way helped move each/all of us into our present commitments, relationships, work, and interests.

But to remember is not only not to forget. To remember is to put back together that which has been dismembered, torn violently into pieces on the basis of fear, greed, hatred, competition, and denial. To remember those whose lives, bodies, spirits, and hearts have been broken is to call them and bring them, by the power of the One whose name is Love, into solidarity with us. We stand with them bonded by God, as lovers and workers together in this world on behalf of one another, ourselves and the Holy Spirit. The act of human love, our mirror to its divine resource, is justice making, the building of right, mutual relations between and among ourselves.

*Revision of a sermon preached at Episcopal Divinity School, on All Saints Day, 1983.

For any one to suffer lack of food, other creature comforts, or dignity, which is what the vast majority of God's people suffer, is for the whole human family to be dismembered. As we gather today to remember Jesus Christ at the Holy Table, we actually circle round this table to embody our commitment to remember a dismembered body: our own and that of all creation, the Body of Christ.

I was so offended by the collect for All Saints' Day that we did not pray it as it is written. This is how it began:

> Almighty God, you have knit together your elect in one com-
> munion of fellowship in the mystical body of your Son Christ our
> Lord . . .[2]

The doctrine of "election," however interpreted, can be postulated only on an assumption that God has chosen certain people and not others to participate in the "mystical" body of Christ. Why must our faith rest on the grounds of exclusivity and special privilege? More to the point, *can* our faith stand on these grounds? I believe not. Our God, the One whom Jesus loved, does not pick and choose, select, elect, set apart, lift up certain groups of people, or individuals, to be "godlike" or "saintly." God chose us all, Christians and Jews and Moslems and wicca and other so-called pagan peoples of all races and nations; both genders, men and women who are single, married, lesbian, gayman, heterosexual, celibate, sexually active; in good health and in poor health. God continues to choose us all. We are the ones who elect, select, sort out, and decide in relation to one another where we shall stand and how we shall live as members of this mystical body. This is a very real and very present body of all people, those who have died, and those who are still alive in this world.

As does so much of our Christian tradition, the hymn "For All the Saints"[3] touches some deep affirmation and yearning in many of our souls. At the same time, there is something wrong here. The hymn manages to mislead us. The value of our tradition as Christians lies in the value of being created, the value of human being, and the value and the power of a love that we can share in this world with one another. Is this not at the heart of what we believe the people of Israel and, later, the Jesus-people experienced and left us as a legacy that we can remember? What do we mean when we, yearning for love, peace, justice, courage and compassion in this world here and now in the smallest places of our lives as well as in the most public, turn our hearts to a heavenly "King" and his otherworldly saints, who have gotten where they are by fighting like soldiers to win a crown of gold? What is it that we expect these bedazzled victors to do for us? And why do we turn to them rather than to our neighbors?

I believe in heaven. I believe that those who have died are with us now. I have come to believe that the place to find and get in touch with these saints is wherever we are right now, at every moment of our lives here on this earth. Images of crowns and battles are not only unhelpful images of sainthood, they are, in an imperialistic and militaristic global situation, destructive images that can lead us only further and deeper into the realms of evil, and hence also into perverse theology.

Yet this great hymn of triumph stirs me, and I think not just the perverse me who can readily fancy herself as a female soldier of a warrior god or goddess. I think the hymn touches a chord of vulnerability in me, as a person who mucks along, "feebly struggling," messing up, often confused. The human experience of struggle and weariness was brilliantly real to the author of this hymn. But the Christian doctrine implicit in the lyrics seems to me even more feeble than my efforts and my faith to do the best I can. Throughout the Christian churches we are in urgent need of people, movements, fresh images, and some good revolutionary work to help get us in touch with the saints of God, living and dead, who live and have lived on the streets, in the fields, in the ghettos, in the suburbs, in the classrooms, in the bars, in the hospitals, and in the parish houses. We need people who know that the peacemakers, justicemakers, lovemakers, compassion-bearers, and courageous nonconformists in this world have always been, and are, and will always be the saints of God.

They need not be sought any further away than in those children and other people who still ask questions, those folks who dare to put their ethics above social and ecclesiastical etiquette, those sisters and brothers who swim madly upstream when the currents are carrying everybody else away to the crown of gold in heaven, those persons who know that their own lives are lived most fully when they are living as representatives of us all in our common humanity, those Grenadians and Filipinos and Salvadorans and Nicaraguans and Palestinians and Chileans who have lived and too often have died so that the rest of us could know what it would really mean to be free.

It is for all of these saints, who may be found no further away than the nearest mirror, that I give thanks to God. And it is for all of these saints, many of whom are missing from our human family, that I ask your prayers.

> Clara Elena Cantero
> Elisa del Carmen Escobar
> Eliana Maria Espinosa
> Rosa Elena Morales,
>
> . . . desaparecida.[4]
> Stand here beside us.

11.

Dressed for Priesthood

An Ordination Sermon*

So holy in my head,
Perfect and light in my deare breast,
My doctrine tun'd by Christ, (who is not dead,
But lives in me while I do rest)
Come people; Aaron's drest.[1]

Sisters and brothers, we have come today, in the poetic words of her spiritual mentor, the English poet George Herbert, "to dress" Anne Carroll Fowler for the priesthood of the church, a vocation of peacemaking. To be clothed in these holy garments is the vocation, moreover, not only of ordained priests but of all of us, the whole people of God. It is the vocation that the church, when it is faithful, reflects on behalf of the whole creation, and which the ordained person, when s/he is faithful, reflects on behalf of the church.

These words should not be heard in an exclusive or superior sense. Neither the ordained priest nor other Christians live above the rest of humankind. Even as we celebrate here today, we may be sure that our own future is being lifted up by lovers of gods and goddesses of peace and justice who may themselves be Jews, Muslims, Hindus, Buddhists, or the practitioners of the "old religion" of wise women, wicca. Only if we assume gladly that our way of keeping faith is neither the only nor

*Revision of a sermon preached at the ordination to the priesthood of Anne C. Fowler, poet and teacher, advocate and activist for justice for women, in May 1986.

64

the best way but rather is a good and sufficient way do we stand a prayer of living well into our shared vocation as Christians.

This vision of one universe, one earth, one people, one body with many members is a strong biblical vision of holiness which we must keep ever before us, for our future is surely at stake. The world of God is a fabulous multi-cultured, many-colored tapestry of histories and experiences. We who are Anglicans, Christians, citizens of the United States, well-fed, well-sheltered people are only a tiny portion of our global family. This does not mean that our particular lives and faith do not matter to God or to our brothers and sisters in the world. We matter a great deal. What we envision, pray for, work for, enjoy, despise, or celebrate is of immeasurable value to the world of God. So too are the lives of every person on this planet: every child in Libya, as well as our own daughters and sons; every teacher and *campesina* in Nicaragua, as well as our own neighbors and friends; every father and mother in South Africa, as well as our own parents and loved ones.

Unless we are clear about this, we can neither preach nor comprehend the Word of God as anything except pious babble. Unless we are prepared to examine what it is that we are doing here in this church today, we might as well shut the Bible, lay aside the prayer book as an artifact of Elizabethan religion, and go home. We are citizens of a nation that speaks with bombs, and members of churches that seldom speak at all; and we dare to preach and celebrate the Word of God as a word of peace. Do we realize in what garments we are actually called by God to dress Anne? Do we understand what it means to name her and claim her as someone who must "go for us," drawing us with her into the complexities of making peace, when there is so little peace—either in the world around us or in our own lives, relationships, and dreams? Are we willing to dress not only Anne Fowler but ourselves as well in the peace-making garments of creation, liberation, and sanctification?

"Jesus said, "Peace I leave with you; my peace I give to you; not as the world gives do I give to you." (John 14:27)

If we are members of a community of peace, a peace that the world does not have, we will be a part of the world in a new, creative way.

May you, Anne, and may we, people, be dressed in the evocative cloth of creation. If work is holy, it is cooperative rather than competitive. To be creative in the imago dei has nothing to do with who is "most" creative, "best" in the field, "most likely to succeed," or at the "top" of the human heap. It has everything to do with our creative power in relation to one another, to all earth creatures, and to the earth itself. May you Anne, and may we, people, dare to envision a world in which our creativity is rooted in our shared capacities to give and receive, teach and learn, succeed and fail, speak and listen, and cooperate rather than either dominate or be dominated. There is no more important lesson for anyone to learn than that her own vocation will forever be formed and re-formed by what she is learning, becoming, and doing in relation to others.

From the perspective of human relationships, I am speaking of our capacities to be genuinely intimate with one another, to evoke creativity from one another (the gift of a good teacher), and to be deeply touched and deeply touching people. We are lovers of God and the world because we are vulnerable: open to being changed, transformed, and converted. From a global perspective, I am envisioning a world in which those who sit at the margins of our lives together (or who are kept out altogether) will lead us into God's peace. From either perspective, we must help one another see that the patient has much to teach the doctor, the Palestinian has much to teach the Jew, the gayman or lesbian has much to teach the heterosexual man or woman, the lay person has much to teach the priest about what it means to live, love, lose, gain, weep, and celebrate as people of God in this world. Many who historically have sat at the edges of our lives, many upon whom we have looked down have more to show us than we them about what it means to keep the faith in a God of courage and perseverance. Only insofar as we live in a cooperative matrix are we able to be involved in the ongoing miracle of creation in which, together, we love one another into the future. Mary gave birth to Jesus, and we call him "Christ" because, in his life, we witness the creative reciprocal power of divine/human love: God and humanity brought to new life together. In each moment of our lives in which we love, we give birth to the hope of the world and are no less *theotokos*, God-bearer, giver and recipient of God's grace, than Mary herself.

Jesus said, "Peace I give you . . . not as the world gives."

Because we are called to bring a peace that the world does not give, we must be also justice-makers. We cannot expect reconciliation without attending to the violence and injustices which every false peace is meant to conceal and deal. *Thus, may you, Anne, and may we, people, be dressed for this occasion in the garments of liberation.* May the world and church we strive to co-create be an arena, not of a false quiescence or passivity which passes for "spirituality," but rather of a sturdy spirituality that requires justice-making. For not only are we members of one Body, we are called to live as such—to live in right relation to one another. Our Christian vocation involves an ongoing hunger after righteousness, an unending quest for basic conditions for survival, well-being, and dignity for all people. The church morally cannot sleep while the world burns. When the prophet Jeremiah and others lament, " 'Peace, peace,' when there is no peace" (Jer. 6:14; 8:11), they are acknowledging that wherever there is no justice, there is no peace. There can be no peace—between white racists and people of color, between battered women and their mates, between the wealthiest nation in the history of the world (our own) and those who are poor at home and abroad. There can be no peace. And no church, no priest, no one on God's earth can make peace in the context of injustice. Thus, peace-makers must be justice-makers.

May you, Anne, may we, people, be vested in the courage to rock some boats, offend some sensibilities, prick some consciences, speak, insist, and persevere when most people around us would rather that we lay off. And let us remember that, if a day goes by when we ourselves are not challenged by some voice—be it angry and demanding or still and small—to shape up and stand for justice in even the most private places of our own lives, we are not listening well to the voice of God. All of our lives are broken by economic, sexual, racial, gender, religious, and national greed, and by other structures of injustice. We are all sinners. Our vocation as people of God is to confess our sin against God and our neighbor (for all practical purposes, the same sin) and "go and sin no more." Though we are stuck in what Augustine called the "damned mass" and will continue individually to be broken and hurt, as well as breaking and hurting others, we have a spiritual mandate to struggle against injustices in our own lives and in the larger life of the church, the nation, the world.

May you, Anne, and may we, people, persevere in the struggle for justice, well aware that just as the builders of the spectacular York Minster, the legendary Canterbury Cathedral, and Europe's other great cathedrals did not live to see the outcome of their own work, we here will not see the full harvest of the seeds we now sow. But if we sow them with conviction, in the spirit of love, and if we realize ourselves connected to those who went before and those who will come after, we will know that whatever small measure we can do on behalf of justice in our own time and place is enough.

Jesus said, "Peace I give you."

May you, Anne, and may we, people, be dressed in the garments of sanctification, themselves the vestments of peace. May you, may we, be filled with the peace that passes understanding, clothed with the power that enables us to go forth rejoicing in the vocation we share. Anne, your own historical, spiritual mentor, George Herbert, realized, as all good poets and priests do, the mysterious ambiguities in which we live. Good ministry, like good poetry, reflects the human experience of ambiguity. We are living and dying, created and creative, sinners and liberators, with roots in both human and divine life.

As such we are dressed in the garments of Christ, clothed in a nondualistic apprehension of a world in which God, humanity, and all earth creatures are involved with one another. Vested in this manner, we see that the Spirit is not above, better than, or separate from the flesh, and that God's world is not set apart from our own. Clothed in the sacramental vestments of this "terrible good," we begin to realize that we eat and drink of the body and blood not simply of one man who died for us, but of all women and men who live and die for us, those whose lives are on the line so that we and all creatures in God's world may have a future. In celebrating the holy mysteries, we share the body and blood of the people of God, which is the Body of God. We share ourselves—our fully human being—as we are created to be, in the image of God; we share that for which Jesus died and was raised again. In celebrating the body of Christ, we lift up and rejoice in our Body/ourselves together.

These garments of creation, liberation and sanctification are the garments of the Holy Trinity. To be trinitarian people is to participate in the ongoing creation, liberation, and sanctification of the world and, in so doing, to be ever more created, liberated, and sanctified ourselves. The ground we share in this world is holy ground. The only way we can defile it is to forget that we share it.

To perceive ourselves and the world of God through a trinitarian lens is to see the sacred as three-dimensional and deep in complexity, rather than as flat and shallow. It is to see God in sexuality, as a sensual, throbbing, yearning being rather than as a sanctimonious, droll blanket of condemnation. It is also to hear God's passion for justice in relationship as over against the shallowness and emptiness of relationship in which there is little or no love.

To live trinitarian lives is to hear the Word of God as stereophonic sound rather than unchanging monotone—to realize, for example, in relation to the issue of abortion, that the voice of God is infinitely more varied, morally thoughtful, and reticent in its tendency to judge than the Roman Catholic hierarchy and a number of Episcopal moralists will dare to admit.

To be vested in the robes of a trinitarian God rather than in those of a secret society of patronizing fathers and obedient sons is to be clothed in the awareness that *to love others is to see the face of God in both self and other.* We see God in others, and in ourselves. Moreover we see that the Spirit of God is manifest in every act of love, every moment of justice-making with courage and compassion, in which we are able to catch a glimpse of God in both ourselves and others. God is revealed as Lover and Beloved and as the creative, liberating, and sanctifying Spirit that draws us together in right relation.

May you, Anne, and may we, people, be blessed with an ever-deepening knowledge that Christ is, has been all along, and will be forever, the relational dynamic of love in which that which we believe to be divine and that which we experience as human coalesce on behalf of the creation, liberation, and sanctification of the world. The Jesus story tells us that this love is, finally, indestructible. Come people, let us be dressed.

12.

Naming Evil for What It Is*
William Stringfellow
1928–1985

It was the summer of 1962. The setting was a conference center tucked away high in the Blue Ridge Mountains of North Carolina, an old, rustic lodge with a southern-style veranda on which we kids grouped to strum guitars and belt out rounds of rowdy church songs. The occasion was the annual Senior High Conference, which drew white kids from across the Southeastern Province of the Episcopal church, and focused each year on a topic such as "The Making of a Christian"; always an edifying-sounding excuse for a reunion on the mountain where we could play underwater "footsie" with those on whom we had crushes.

On this particular occasion the unlikely topic was "The Wrath of God and Racial Bigotry." The speaker appeared unimpressive: a white, short, stocky man with a crew cut, a tight walk, and an expressionless stone-face. Like the rest of the kids, I was prepared to plop down unenthusiastically in his audience, pay as little attention as I could politely get away with, and bide time until our chance to return to the lake, the music, and each other.

I will never forget William Stringfellow. When this most unremarkable looking man opened his mouth, the wrath of God hit full-force. For the first time in my sixteen years, I was slapped in my soul with the fact that, like everyone in the room, I was living in the sin of white

*Revision of sermon preached at Episcopal Divinity School, Cambridge, Massachusetts, March 5, 1985. An earlier version of this sermon appeared as "Requiem for a Theologian, Advocate, Friend" in *The Witness*, April 1985. Reprinted with permission.

racism. He named it evil, and he named the Episcopal church responsible for it. He made clear his understanding that by the "Episcopal church" he meant *us*, a run-of-the-mill bunch of white, high-school students. We were part of the spiritual problem unless we were involved actively in its concrete, historical, political solution.

William Stringfellow was the first white person I heard condemn unequivocally the evil of racism and the church's active involvement in its perpetuation. A lawyer and layman, he was also the first Episcopal church leader in my experience who took the people of God, including a bunch of teenagers, seriously enough to hold us responsible for both the ghastly character of evil in our society and for the spirit-filled possibility of its undoing.

He was an irascible character. He did not seem to give a whit whether we liked him. He did not pamper us emotionally, tell us jokes, flirt with us, or manipulate us by guilt-tripping or spiritually baiting us into admiring him, ourselves, or people of color. He did not use palatable religious language. He did not say that our primary business as Christians was to pray for racial justice. He did not cajole us by suggesting that our call was to reconcile, unify, educate, or pacify the people of God. He laid it out to us: racism was our problem. Its solution was God's—and *our* spiritual—business. Our only business as Christians was to stand for God regardless of the consequences.

I look back on that conference as a turning point in my life. Never since have I been able to believe that we should be spiritual instead of political. William Stringfellow was my first theological mentor. He died after a long, dreadful, metabolic disease had wracked his body unmercifully and left him only a bare skeleton of the chunky little prophet who had once upon a time changed my life. Upon his death, the Episcopal church—indeed, the Christian church and, more broadly, the religious community in the United States—lost one of its most unequivocal and irrepressible voices for justice within and beyond the church. Stringfellow should be given a day in our liturgical calendar, but this is not likely to happen soon because neither his tone nor his message was as sweet as we expect those of our religious heroes to be.

Today's lessons help illuminate Stringfellow's theology. Like his own theological mentor, Karl Barth, Stringfellow understood the collective character of human sin. A vintage neo-orthodox preacher and writer, Stringfellow understood God's condemnation of Israel as the exact moral equivalent of God's condemnation of the United States for the same sins today:

> Ah, sinful nation,
>   a people laden with iniquity,
> offspring of evildoers
>   children who deal corruptly!
> They have forsaken the Sovereign . . .
>   they are utterly estranged.

>   (Isa. 1:4)

This was Stringfellow's message to our nation, whether the specific evil was racism, sexism, the imperialistic violence wrought by us in Southeast Asia two decades ago, the evil that we reap in Central America today, or simply the building of our nation and our lives on "lies, secrets, and silence" (Adrienne Rich). He believed that human societies are corrupt and that we are faced with a choice of standing for or against God in every situation. And how do we know where God stands? The Bible, Stringfellow believed, is clear: God stands with every human being whose survival or dignity is thwarted by the greed, indifference, and violence that are embedded in our systems of racial, sexual, and economic stratification. When arrested in 1970 for harboring Dan Berrigan, Catholic peace activist and fugitive, Stringfellow's response was that he was just a Christian doing his duty.

Perhaps more than any other Episcopalian of our time, Stringfellow's biting, sardonic critiques were leveled not only against our nation but also against our church. Much in what he believed to be the righteously indignant, angry spirit of Jesus, Stringfellow despised religiosity:

> . . . they preach, but do not practice;
> . . . they do all their deeds to be seen by others;
> . . . they love the place of honor at feasts.

>   (from Matthew 23)

In Stringfellow's judgment, these charges had to be made against the current leadership of the Episcopal church who, he believed, stand among us today in exactly the same morally untenable posture as the pompous, pious legalists of first-century Palestine stood among Jesus and his friends. Presiding Bishop Allin[1] could only wish, I dare say, that just as the religious people of Jesus' time dismissed him, contemporary Episcopalians would write William Stringfellow off as a fanatic and would close our ears to his scathing indictments of our empty rituals.

Twelve years after my first encounter with Stringfellow we met again, this time around the events leading up to and following the ordination of eleven of us women in Philadelphia in 1974. Stringfellow offered to be our legal counsel during the two years of our exile from the church's officially ordained priesthood. During this time he served as attorney for those male priests brought to ecclesiastical trial for having invited women priests to celebrate the Eucharist in their parishes. Stringfellow stood with us during the 1974 meeting of the House of Bishops in Chicago, at which time the bishops declared our ordination to be "invalid"—that we were not, in fact, priests. Stringfellow stated publicly his conviction that the bishops' judgment was null and void legally, morally, and pastorally.

Two years later, Stringfellow was with the ordained women priests during the 1976 General Convention in Minneapolis, at which, while women's ordination was approved, the House of Bishops voted that the "irregularly" ordained women would have to be "conditionally re-ordained." After meeting with us, Stringfellow evidently went to the bishops and set them on notice. He told them that we, the women priests, would not be re-ordained, conditionally or otherwise. Recognizing trouble, the House of Bishops reversed its ruling and voted unanimously to allow the already ordained women to be simply "recognized" by our own bishops and thus by the church at large.

No one should try to "imitate" her mentors. I did not agree with the radicality of Stringfellow's neo-orthodox dualism. Thus, I could not share his unmitigated condemnation of all human systems as necessarily corrupt and of so many of our leaders, such as the presiding bishop (for whom I also had no great fondness), as depraved. Conversely, it was clear to me that Stringfellow was puzzled by the feminist commitment he found in me and others around him, even as he struggled alongside women priests as our advocate. I know, from one of our last conversations several years before his death, that Bill Stringfellow did not understand why I came out as a lesbian. It seemed to him a morally sound but politically foolish thing to do. The personal for him was not always political. He chose not to call attention to his love for his companion Anthony until toward the end. At that point he and Anthony had nothing left to lose—except that which Bill knew for sure he would not lose: the love of those whose friend and advocate he had been and of the God in whose realm he now lives freely.

I thank God for the life and work of William Stringfellow—friend, advocate, theologian.

13.

*To Comfort Those Who Mourn**

J. Brooke Mosley
1915–1988

The Spirit of the Sovereign God is upon me
because God has anointed me
to bring good tidings to the afflicted . . .
to proclaim liberty to the captives . . .
to comfort all who mourn . . .
to give them a garland instead of ashes . . .
the mantle of praise instead of a faint spirit;
that they may be called oaks of righteousness.

(Isa. 61:1–3)

The rector of this parish, Rodger Broadley, tells me that from this pulpit in the mid-nineteenth century his predecessor, the Reverend Mr. Tyeng, became one of the first non-Quakers in Philadelphia to preach an antislavery sermon, for which he was forthwith fired. I am reasonably confident that this particular historical legacy is one of the reasons Brooke Mosley asked that his own funeral take place here. Brooke wanted his own life, and ours, to be linked actively and historically with those who have struggled for justice.

When I asked myself, "What would Brooke want me to do this morning?" an answer reflecting the spirit of Brooke's own ministry

*Revision of a sermon preached at a service of thanksgiving for the life of J. Brooke Mosley at The Church of St. Luke and the Epiphany in Philadelphia, Pennsylvania, on March 8, 1988. An earlier revision appeared in *The Witness*, May 1988. Reprinted with permission.

came to me in the words of the prophet Isaiah: Brooke would want me to comfort those who mourn. To comfort means literally to strengthen those who are here to celebrate the life and mourn the death of our good friend. Such comforting is what Brooke wanted for his funeral—what he wanted to be able to do in death—because it is what Brooke tried to do in life: to strengthen us to strengthen others, to empower us to be a wellspring from which the brokenhearted, the abused, the victimized, and the outcast may draw strength and, in so doing, become comforters—providers of strength—to others.

This powerful line of continuity, at once historical and mystical, social, and spiritual, is what Brooke Mosley stood for. It is what he understood the Christian church to ideally be. And it is, I am certain, what he wished to give us in his dying: a clear, unequivocal charge to stand together in the justice-seeking line of continuity, and to live together in the ecumenical and often secular spirit of the prophets. We who are Christian may also recognize this spirit-filled line of justice-seeking continuity as "the way, the truth, and the life" of God, which was revealed to our religious forebears and, through them, to us in the life of Jesus of Nazareth (see John 14:6a).

I was moved to read in the *Philadelphia Inquirer* about what sounded like two of Brooke's early "conversion" experiences. The first was the experience of working in a cemetery and watching poor people bring expensive bouquets to the gravesites. The second was working as a salesman in a large retail store until he learned that regular employees had been laid off so that he and other students could be hired more cheaply.

Thinking about these turning points and about Brooke's life and ministry in general, I was reminded of Frederick Denison Maurice, a nineteenth-century English theologian, teacher, activist, advocate of women's rights, champion of workingmen and workingwomen, and a founder of the Christian Socialist movement in England. He was fired from his post as Professor of Theology at Kings College, London, ostensibly because of an essay in which he rejected the very notion of "eternal damnation" at the hands of a loving God.

What F. D. Maurice and Brooke Mosley had in common, besides an obvious similarity of commitments and interests, was that, as white males with access to economic privilege, they used their racial, gender, and class privilege on behalf of those who did not and do not have it. I think, to be honest, that this could not have been easy for either F. D. Maurice or Brooke Mosley, nor for any who have the privilege of choosing to cast our lots with those who do not have this same privilege, this same range of options from which to decide what to do with their lives.

It could not have been easy for Brooke Mosley to give up his sales job on behalf of laid-off workers.

It could not have been easy in 1973 for Brooke to walk out before the Eucharist in a service in the Cathedral of St. John the Divine with five women deacons who had been refused ordination moments earlier.

It could not have been easy for Brooke to be castigated publicly by a number of the most powerful members of the faculty of Union Theological Seminary (New York), who interpreted his insistence on the priority of the admission of large number of blacks, Hispanics, and women—and his desire to hold the seminary accountable to the needs of New York City—as antithetical to their understanding of "academic excellence."

It could not have been easy for Brooke Mosley, on his pilgrimages to Harrisburg, Pennsylvania, to testify on behalf of a woman's right to choose abortion, to pass through groups of hecklers who were shouting, "Killer bishop!"

It could not have been easy to have been one of so very few Episcopal bishops to stand publicly and proudly with openly gaymen and lesbian priests, laity, and citizens as our ally and advocate.

It could not have been easy for a sixty-five-year-old Anglo to learn Spanish so that he could, in his words, "confirm the children of North Philadelphia in their own language."

It could not have been easy for Brooke Mosley to have spent virtually his entire adult life learning how to surrender privilege in order to genuinely be able to comfort the brokenhearted, the afflicted, and those who mourn.

It could not have been easy for Brooke Mosley because it is not easy for anyone to learn by living all that is involved in losing one form of security in order to gain another far deeper and more trustworthy form.

Yet "what you sow does not come to life until it dies" (1 Cor. 15:36b). Paul's reference here is not only, I believe, to the resurrection of the body after we die but also to the resurrection of the spirit while we live. In order to come to life among us, God's Spirit requires that we learn to surrender our privilege, whatever sets us above and apart from others. Only insofar as we do this can we be empowered genuinely to comfort one another. This way, this truth, this life—the way of Miriam and Moses, the truth of Mary and Jesus, the life of Harriet Tubman and Martin Luther King, Jr., the way of martyred Salvadoran Archbishop Oscar Romero and assassinated gay rights leader Harvey Milk—is never easy.

I have an image of Brooke Mosley striding toward a microphone at the 1973 General Convention in Louisville; striding down the hall at Union Seminary; striding across the sand toward his sailboat in South Dartmouth; chest barrelled, body upright, chin up, jaw set, bearing purposeful and sometimes very stubborn. It is to me a likely image of one whom Isaiah might well call an "oak of righteousness"—formidable. But we must realize that whereas oaks are sturdy trees with deep roots, which is their strength, they do not bend easily, which can be a problem.

It was not easy for Brooke to bend in new directions—and yet he did. In spite of some fierce ambivalences, in spite of his own feelings sometimes, Brooke Mosley learned how to change. It is not easy for any of us with deep roots and sturdy convictions to change. Yet we must if we are to live in the Sacred Spirit of One who calls us daily into new occasions to love this earth and all living creatures. Brooke Mosley, as much as anyone I have ever known, loved learning, and he loved his way into learning how to change.

It would be untrue to the spirit of our brother not to mention here in his memory the vitality of humor in the work of justice. Humor is not basically about "funny things." Humor is about keeping things in perspective. It is rooted in an ability to see ourselves and one another as we really are and to enjoy what we see!

This perspective enabled Brooke Mosley, as it does anyone who shares it, to exercise a fervent commitment to justice with an equally strong sense of compassion and a free spirit, not taking either himself or others so seriously as to lose sight of the fact that we are born into this world to enjoy ourselves and one another. This is our common birthright—the right of every person—to be happy, to laugh, to play, to have humane work and leisure time. Brooke enjoyed himself and others, which is what enabled so many of us to enjoy him.

In this spirit, his remarkable wife and life-companion, Betty, has asked me to share with you the story of how their daughter Rimmie managed to get Brooke's body back from New York City, where he had collapsed and died.

The task of having her father's body returned to Pennsylvania fell to Rimmie, who is a teacher in New York. Rimmie learned from a woman at the Office of the Medical Examiner that the body could not be released for return until after an autopsy. Rimmie said that the family did not need or desire an autopsy, to which the woman responded that it was mandatory—except in cases where there were religious proscriptions against it. When, like an oak, Rimmie held out against the autopsy, the woman said simply, "Okay, I'll fix it."

Later in the day, when Rimmie returned for the body and looked at the document authorizing its release, she saw that it read:

> *name:* J. Brooke Mosley
> *occupation:* Episcopal bishop
> *religion:* Jewish

Brooke, who struggled actively against the anti-Semitic implications and innuendoes in so much of Christian doctrine, is bound to be enjoying this story of his own passage into a more fully ecumenical and universal dimension of God's realm!

Corita Kent, at one time a Sister of the Immaculate Heart and later a Boston-based artist famous for her powerful paintings against the Vietnam War, chose her own epitaph several months before her death in 1985:

> She whom we love
> and lose
> is no longer
> where she was before
>
> She is now
> wherever we are.
>
> (St. John Chrysostom)

So too with Brooke Mosley:

> He is no longer
> where he was
>
> He is now
> wherever we are.

14.

*Ahead of Her Time, Yet Fully in It**
Nelle Morton
1902–1987

Nelle Morton showed me Wisdom: she lived ahead of her time yet fully in it. This she was able to do, I am convinced, because she grew from her roots rather than attempting to lop herself off from the racism and sexism which soured the soil she knew best. Thus rooted forever in her white Southern Christian heritage, Nelle joined the struggle in the world and church against white-race supremacy and male-gender hegemony with the special tenacity reserved for those who know most intimately the demons with which they contend.

Similarly, Nelle's work as a scholar was radical, drawing us toward the root of intellectual excellence—the holistic, multidimensional character of epistemology, or how we know what we know. Her pioneering demonstration of art, images, and metaphor as foundational to intelligent theological discourse bears a wisdom essential to theological creativity. It is a lesson neither understood nor valued by most Christian theologians and teachers.

Amidst the empowering legacy Nelle Morton has left us, the most challenging of her gifts to her younger sisters may be our recognition that the Goddess can live and thrive wherever we are. This wisewoman knew that the journey of the Sacred is not contained within or without the various complicated institutions of our lives. Nelle knew

---

*Revision of an essay written upon hearing of Nelle Morton's death. An earlier version of this essay appeared as "Nelle Morton Journeys Home" in *Christianity and Crisis*, September 14, 1987.

that Wisdom moves with us to the extent that we move together on behalf of a more fully just and decent and lovely world.

She called us to come together, act together, celebrate together and, when we must, suffer together. She lusted after life and love and, in this playful, sensual Spirit, she wanted us to enjoy ourselves. Nelle Morton believed in womanpower, in herself, in women, and not only in white, middle-strata, or Euroamerican women. Nelle's vision was global, multicultured, and multicolored. Nelle envisioned the possibilities of shared sisterly power. She saw us as the hope for the world.

Nelle convinced me that the eternal Spirit of womanpower is not merely another face of the patriarchal deity YHWH. For her, and increasingly for me, the Goddess is an altogether different source of creative and liberating power. In this Spirit, Nelle emobdied an altogether different sort of intellectual power from that of most of her ecclesial and academic colleagues. She felt, not only "thought." She imagined, not only "knew." Nelle did not merely argue theological truth; she laughed and cried and bled and dared to dream. She was involved in the life of the Sacred, not a "spokeswoman for God" or an "objective" observer of divine life.

Her legacy bears two questions that will determine finally the value of that legacy: What shall we do with what Nelle Morton left us? and How shall we do it? However we answer, Nelle Morton will be around, close to the heart of Wisdom, all rolled up in the movement of the Sacred toward the justice, peace, and womanpower in which she believed so fiercely.

15.

Crossing the River*

And she stood far off on the bank of the river.

And she said, "For what do I go to this far land which no one has ever reached? Oh, I am alone! I am utterly alone!"

And Reason, that old man, said to her, "Silence! what do you hear?"

And she listened intently, and she said, "I hear a sound of feet, a thousand times ten thousand and thousands of thousands, & they beat this way!"

He said, "They are the feet of those that shall follow you. Lead on! make a track to the water's edge! Where you stand now, the ground will be beaten flat by ten thousand times ten thousand feet." And he said, "Have you seen the locusts how they cross a stream? First one comes down to the water-edge, and it is swept away, and then another comes and then another, and at last with their bodies piled up a bridge is built and the rest pass over."

She said, "And of those that come first, some are swept away, and are heard of no more; their bodies do not even build the bridge?"

"And are swept away, and are heard of no more—and what of that?" he said.

"And what of that—" she said. "They make a track to the water's edge."

"They make a track to the water's edge—" And she said, "Over that bridge which shall be built with our bodies, who will pass?"

He said, "The entire human race."

And the woman grasped her staff.

And I saw her turn down that dark path to the river.[1]

*Revision of a sermon preached at a service in celebration of women's ministries, the National Cathedral, Washington, D.C., May 26, 1984.

"Have you seen the locusts how they cross a stream?" wrote Olive Schreiner, South African writer, suffragist, and peace activist. I know of no stronger image for the servanthood to which Jesus says that we, like he, are called, than that of the locusts who attempt to cross the river and, in so doing, make a bridge for others.

On July 29, 1974, eleven white, well-fed, well-educated women in the United States crossed a river.[2] We were upheld in our journey by the bodies, blood, dreams, and disappointments of countless women in history, most of whose names and stories have been purposely purged from our common story. On that grand summer day in North Philadelphia, we processed on the bodies of those many priestly deaconesses and nuns whose work made ours possible. We journeyed, buoyed up by the dreams of laywomen for a fullness of personhood and participation in the church. We walked in the blood of racial/ethnic women and poor women who have labored historically in this and other lands for a measure of justice, a labor that most of us here today cannot comprehend fully. On that electric day in the Church of the Advocate, we forged a course on the disappointments of our mothers and grandmothers, our foresisters of all generations, races, and religions who had gone before us in the pilgrimage to lands that flow with milk and honey and to tables set with bread and wine.

Please do not imagine that the "Philadelphia Eleven" (and a year later the "Washington Four")[3] were individuals simply answering personal calls from God. An individual's personal choice is moral only insofar as it represents the well-being of others. The first Episcopal women priests, like the women struggling before us, were representatives of a fully human/fully divine movement across rivers which threaten to drown the family of God, and perhaps God Herself, in mighty undertows of callous indifference to human well-being. Without our people, past and present, and without our commitments to future generations, we would have drowned. Without our awareness that it was, in fact, others on whose bodies and blood we were fed for our journey, we would have been lonely strangers to God and God's people. Without our willingness to be part of the bridge upon which others might one day travel safely, we would have been stunned into bitter disbelief and resentment.

The efficacy and power of Christian vocation simmers in the realization that only insofar as we are together can we sustain our vision, our energies, and our patience. It is through such solidarity that we realize that our vision of what a just world and church will be and is becoming already is a vision of God's realm.

The intensity of this vision of God's realm may blind us with its brilliance, yet we see. Our participation in the common-wealth of joy and pride in all that is good will cost us, yet we celebrate. The sacred space in which courage and compassion are one may confound us, yet we know. We know that our vision of what the church must be if it is to be worth a moment of either human or divine time calls us to be both its bearers and its fulfillment; both *theotokos*, the bearer, and *corpus christa*, the born. We know that together, in solidarity, we are she: women and men, older and younger, people of different races and cultures and religions, we are she. Lesbians and gaymen, heterosexual men and women, married and single, with our diverse gifts and our divergent interests, in our shared commitment to human well-being, we are she. In our own Christian faith we know that in our shared commitment to human well-being, we are she: bearer and born, mother and child. We are the Christa.[4] In Nicaragua we see and experience a people who know that living or dead, all who have been a part of the struggle are *presente!* In this tradition I close remembering particular women and inviting each to be present with us in her own way:

I remember Sue Hiatt, who led the small movement for women's ordination in the Episcopal church. Without Sue, we would not be here today in this tenth-anniversary celebration of women priests, for there would have been no Philadelphia ordination and in all likelihood no women priests in the United States. Many of us call Sue our bishop. Blessed be her name.

I remember our beloved late sister Jeannette Piccard, who makes me smile to this day. I remember how in 1973 when the presiding bishop-elect continued to refer to a group of us women deacons as "girls," seventy-nine-year-old Jeannette pounded her cane on the floor, slapped him on the knee, smiled, and reprimanded him sharply. "No, sonnyboy, not a girl. I'm old enough to be your mama!" Blessed be her name.

I remember Alice Walker, who, in *The Color Purple*, comes as close as any other theologian I have read to laying to rest once and for all the notion that an old white man in the sky is going to do much good for anybody in a racist/sexist society, except for those white men who collude with him and thereby work their way up. Blessed be her name.

I remember Ellen Barrett, an unapologetically woman-loving woman, whose integrity stunned the church and whose courage enabled others of us to come out as witnesses to the moral power of a love that is revealed, not hidden, and to a way of being in the world that is chosen, not imposed. Blessed be her name.

I remember Mother Jones, who lived for her people, the poor. Crusty and irascible, in every white-patriarchal, capitalistic sense an "irregular" woman, Mother Jones summed up the gist of what we must do: "Pray for the dead, and fight like hell for the living."[5] Blessed be her name.

Finally, I thank God for you and for our common life. Blessed be.

Notes

CHAPTER 1. *Doing Feminist Liberation Christology*

1. Audre Lorde, "The Master's Tools Will Never Dismantle the Master's House" in *Sister Outsider: Essays and Speeches* (Trumansburg, N.Y.: Crossing, 1984), 112.

2. I am especially grateful to Kelly Brown, Beverly Harrison, Peg Huff, Pat Shechter, Ann Wetherilt, and Delores Williams.

3. Since childhood I have been more interested in images of Jesus as brother and friend than of Christ as King and Lord (save a brief excursus as a teenager into Anglo-Catholicism). I also hoped that through this paper I would be able to explore why it is that most christology bores me while the Jesus story has always generated my passion.

4. All theology is to some extent reactive against its author's perceptions of earlier theological distortions, excesses, or errors, such as the reaction of such "crisis" theologians as Karl Barth (1886–1968) against the relativism of such liberals as Albrecht Ritschl (1822–1889), and the reaction of liberation theologian Dorothee Soelle (1928–   ) in one of her first books, *Political Theology* (1971), against the individualism of existential theologian Rudolf Bultmann (1884–1976).

5. Cf. Rosemary Radford Ruether, *Sexism and God-Talk: Toward a Feminist Theology* (Boston: Beacon Press, 1983), esp. 72–92; Joan L. Griscom, "On Healing the Nature/History Split in Feminist Thought," pp. 85–98, and Toinette M. Eugene, "While Love is Unfashionable," in Barbara Hilkert Andolsen, Christine E. Gudorf, and Mary D. Pellauer, eds., *Women's Consciousness, Women's Conscience* (Minneapolis: Winston, 1985), 121–41, for helpful discussions of dualism as a theological and ethical problem.

6. I am aware that for many "Christian women of different colors, cultures, and classes," Jesus/Christ is redemptive in that he "saves" them from a sense of personal despair. From the perspective of liberation theology, however, redemption (or salvation) involves the ongoing creation of justice. It is within the context of this process that personal salvation (from despair, loneliness, meaninglessness, etc.) is available.

7. This point is made with compassion and clarity by Tom F. Driver, *Christ in a Changing World: Toward an Ethical Christology* (New York: Crossroad, 1981).

8. I must confess that in studying christology I find myself awash in a sea of sexist language. I respond to it much the way I would to tobacco if, as a reformed smoker, I were to take another cigarette. Does classical christology lock us necessarily into the relation between Father and Son as the locus of universal redemption? In writing this essay, I decided not to fight "the sexist habit" but rather go with it on a hunch that, in its classical terms, christology is actually an exercise in patriarchal logic.

In its classical terms, christology has been an effort to hold together the human Jesus (a Jewish male) and his divine "nature." It has been together that his "humanity" and "divinity" have been "Christ." I believe that Jesus' human-ness—including (though not limited to) his maleness—has been basic to classi-cal christology. Such christology, imaging Christ, cannot become separated from the historical figure who was in fact a man. I continue to believe this is basic to classical christological discourse and is one reason that classical christology is a dead theological language. In this essay, when I refer to the Jesus Christ of classical christology, I purposely am using the masculine pro-nouns as well as the word "man." I do not mean it generically.

9. See H. S. Reimarus (1694–1768), *On the Intention of Jesus* (Leiden: E. J. Brill, 1970); and David Friedrich Strauss (1808–1874), *The Life of Jesus Critically Examined* (1831–1838; Philadelphia: Fortress Press, 1972).

10. In this broad inclusive sense, "the historical Jesus" or "Jesus of history" is assumed by all Christian liberation theologians to be foundational to christology.

11. I. Carter Heyward, *The Redemption of God: A Theology of Mutual Relation* (Lanham, Md.: Univ. Press of America, 1982), 31.

12. Friedrich Schleiermacher, *The Christian Faith* (1812; Philadelphia: For-tress Press, 1976).

13. Rudolf Bultmann, *Jesus Christ and Mythology* (New York: Charles Scribner's Sons, 1958).

14. Frederick Denison Maurice, *Theological Essays* (1853; London: James Clarke, 1957); *Kingdom of Christ (or, Hints to a Quaker Respecting the Principles, Constitution and Ordinances of the Catholic Church)*, 2 vols. (1838–42; London: SCM Press, 1958).

15. E.g., Richard Hurrell Froude (1803–1836), John Keble (1792–1866), John Henry Newman (1801–1890), and Edward Bouverie Pusey (1801–1882).

16. Consider the following passage from the Right Reverend Desmond Tutu's *Hope and Suffering: Sermons and Speeches* (Grand Rapids: Wm. B. Eerdmans, 1985), 84–85:

"The Gospel of Jesus Christ is a many-splendoured thing, a jewel with several facets. In [certain] situations[s] . . . , the aspect of the Gospel that will be relevant is the Gospel as reconciliation. [But] if you are oppressed and the victim of exploitation, then the Gospel for you will be liberation. . . .

"Black and White Christians look at Jesus Christ and they see a different

reality. It is almost like beauty, which is said to be in the eye of the be-
holder. . . .

"Christianity knows nothing about pie in the sky when you die, or concern
for man's soul only. That would be a travesty of the religion of Jesus of
Nazareth, who healed the sick, fed the hungry, etc. . . . *Jesus showed that for the
spiritual God, His Kingdom must have absolute centrality; but precisely because that was
so, because He turned Godwards, He of necessity had to be turned manwards. He was the
Man for others precisely because He was first and foremost the Man of God"* (emphasis
mine).

17. Maurice, "The Son of God," in *Theological Essays*, 81.

18. Ibid.

19. Ibid.

20. Albert Schweitzer, *The Quest of the Historical Jesus: A Critical Study of Its
Program from Reimarus to Wrede*, ed. James Robinson (1906; New York: Mac-
millan & Co., 1968), 62–67.

21. "Alienation" is a term in Marxist theory which denotes "negation of
productivity." Erich Fromm writes, "Alienation (or 'estrangement') means, for
Marx, that man does not experience himself as the acting agent in his grasp of
the world, but that the world (nature, others, and he himself) remain alien to
him. They stand above and against him as objects, even though they may be
objects of his own creation. Alienation is essentially experiencing the world and
oneself passively, receptively, as the subject separated from the object" *(Marx's
Concept of Man* [New York: Ungar, 1961], 44).

22. This reference is specifically to the bronze sculpture "Christa" by English artist Edwina Sandys.

23. The development of this idea was initiated in the third century by
Cyprian, Bishop of Carthage, a student of Tertullian. Trying to secure the
unity of the church in an era of its persecution by the Roman state, Cyprian
identified the presence of the church with the person of the bishop. "Letters,"
66.8, in *The Fathers of the Church (A New Translation)*, vol. 51, (Washington,
D.C.: Catholic Univ. of America Press, 1964), 228–29.

24. This is the primary theme of Tom F. Driver's christological work *(Christ
in a Changing World)*. Tom Driver was my teacher and mentor at Union Seminary in New York. I continue to appreciate and learn from his christological
wisdom.

CHAPTER 2   *Speaking of Christ*

1. On christology from a liberation perspective, see Jon Sobrino, *Christology
at the Crossroads: A Latin American Approach* (New York: Orbis Books, 1978);
Leonardo Boff, *Jesus Christ Liberator: A Critical Christology for Our Time* (New
York: Orbis Books, 1978); José Miranda, *Being and the Messiah: The Message of St.
John* (New York: Orbis Books, 1972); Tom F. Driver, *Christ in a Changing World:*

Toward an Ethical Christology (New York: Crossroad, 1982); James Cone, *For My People: Black Theology and the Black Church* (New York: Orbis Books, 1984); and I. Carter Heyward, *The Redemption of God: A Theology of Mutual Relation* (Lanham, Md.: Univ. Press of America, 1982).

2. Maurice wrote,"Apart from Him, I feel there dwells in me no good thing; but I am sure that I am not apart from Him, nor are you. Nor is any man." (*Theological Essays* [London: James Clarke, 1957], 67.)

3. In *Lux Mundi: A Series of Studies in the Religion of the Incarnation* 6th ed. (London: John Murray, 1890), Charles Gore and others address the tensions between general and special incarnational emphases in Anglicanism. Writing on "The Christian Doctrine of God," Aubrey Moore stated, "Either God is everywhere present in nature, or He is nowhere. He cannot be here and not there. . . . In nature everything must be His work or nothing" (*Lux Mundi*, 99). The incarnational tension between general and special revelation has been reflected more recently in John A. T. Robinson, *Honest to God* (Philadelphia: Westminster Press, 1963), and Durstan R. McDonald, ed., *Myth/Truth of God Incarnate: The Tenth National Conference of Trinity Institute* (Wilton, Conn.: Morehouse-Barlow, 1979).

4. This was my attempt in *The Redemption of God*. Two other Episcopal feminists who have addressed christological issues are Marjorie Hewitt Suchocki, *God Christ Church: A Practical Guide to Process Theology* (New York: Crossroad, 1982); and Patricia Wilson-Kastner, *Faith, Feminism, and the Christ* (Philadelphia: Fortress Press, 1983).

5. Richard Hooker is required reading to understand "participation" as fundamental to our life as a church. See *The Laws of Ecclesiastical Polity* (London: J. M. Dent, 1954, Book 5, Chap. 51–57). My colleague Fredrica Harris Thompsett has lectured brilliantly on the meaning of "participation" in Hooker. See also John E. Booty on Hooker in *The Spirit of Anglicanism*, ed. William J. Wolf (Wilton, Conn.: Morehouse-Barlow, 1979).

6. See esp. Emily C. Hewitt and Suzanne R. Hiatt, *Women Priests: Yes or No?* (New York: Seabury Press, 1973), for a well-considered treatment of this. A more recent and general historical work of the Episcopal Women's History Project in the U.S. is an important resource. See, e.g., Sandra Hughes Boyd, ed., *Cultivating Our Roots: A Guide to Gathering Church Women's History* (Cincinnati: Forward Movement, 1984). Charles Raven's 1929 text on women and ordained ministry, as critical to the life of the whole people of God, remains a classic. See Raven, *Women and Holy Orders* (1929), with postscript by George G. Swanson (Kansas City, Mo.: The Prospers, 1975). American women are indebted to and in solidarity with the ongoing movement among women in England (Una Kroll, et al.) on behalf of ordination.

7. See Dorothee Soelle, *Christ the Representative: An Essay in Theology After "The Death of God"* (London: SCM Press, 1967); Sobrino, *Christology at the Crossroads*; Heyward, *The Redemption of God;* and Rita Nakashima Brock, "The

Feminist Redemption of Christ" in *Christian Feminism: Visions of a New Humanity*, ed. Judith L. Weidman (San Francisco: Harper & Row, 1984), 55–74.

CHAPTER 4. *Crying in the Wilderness*

1. A reading from the journal of Chris, a man whose partner died of AIDS. Earl E. Shelp, Ronald H. Sutherland, and Peter W. A. Mansell, eds., *AIDS: Personal Stories in Pastoral Perspective* (New York: Pilgrim Press, 1986), 127–29.

CHAPTER 5. *The "Not Yet" of Women's Rights*

1. Resources on the worsening situation of women's lives include Audrey Bronstein, *Triple Struggle: Latin American Peasant Women* (Boston: South End, 1983); Maria Rosa Cutrufelli, *Women of Africa: Roots of Oppression* (London: Zed Books, 1983); Center for National Policy Review staff, *The Feminization of Poverty: Women, Work and Welfare* (Washington, D.C.: Catholic Univ. of America, 1978); *Third World, Second Sex: Women's Struggles and National Liberation*, ed. Miranda Davies (London: Zed Books, 1983); and Chris Kaplan and Vikki Gregory, *The Feminization of Poverty: An Update* (Washington, D.C.: Wider Opportunities for Women, 1983).

2. I am reminded of this when I remember conversations with peasant women in Nicaragua, whose children, once fighting for their lives against the hunger and disease brought on by United States foreign policy implemented by Somoza, now struggle for their lives against the atrocities promulgated by United States-sponsored contras. South Africa is another example of this truth. Think of the black women of South Africa, who are twice victims—of sex and of race. Women were among the sixty-nine massacred in Sharpeville in 1960, and it was mostly women and children who were slaughtered in November, 1985, in Mamelodi, in the shadow of Pretoria.

3. Archbishop Oscar Romero of El Salvador, a defender of human rights, was assassinated as he celebrated Mass in March 1980. Chief Albert Luthuli was elected president of the African National Congress in 1953 and awarded the Nobel Peace Prize in 1961 because of his peaceful resistance to apartheid. He was banned in his own country of South Africa and died accidentally in 1967. Victoria Mxenge, a prominent South African human rights lawyer, was gunned down and hacked to death by unknown assailants in August, 1985, while representing sixteen United Democratic Front leaders on trial for treason. Isaac Muofhe, a South African Lutheran lay preacher, died while in security police custody after his arrest in November, 1981.

CHAPTER 6. *Daring to Discern Divinity*

1. Men and women preparing for ordination in the Episcopal church must take General Ordination Exams. GOEs are meant to offer guidance to those reviewing and recommending the person as to his/her preparation, readiness,

and suitability for ordination. They are given every year during the first week of January.

CHAPTER 7. *Learning to See*

1. *Eyes on the Prize: America's Civil Rights Years*, Episode 3, "Ain't Scared of Your Jails (1960–61)" (Boston: Blackside, 1986). Videotape. Distributed by PBS Video, Alexandria, Va.

CHAPTER 8. *The Spark Is God*

1. Nikos Kazantzakis, *Saviors of God; Spiritual Exercises*, trans. Kimon Friar (New York: Simon & Schuster, 1960), 99.

CHAPTER 9. *Humility*

1. The Right Reverend Emilio Hernandez is the bishop of the Diocese of Cuba.

2. John Newton, *The Journal of a Slave Trader 1750–1754: with Newton's "Thoughts upon the African Slave Trade*," ed. Bernard Martin and Mark Spurrel (London: Epworth Press, 1962), 95.

3. Ibid., 98.

4. For more on the life of John Newton see *Out of the Depths: The Autobiography of John Newton*, introduction by Herbert Lockyear (New Canaan, Conn.: Keats Publishing, 1981); and Newton, *The Journal of a Slave Trader 1750–1754*.

5. Brian H. Edwards, *Through Many Dangers* (Grand Rapids: Evangelical Press, 1975), 177–78.

CHAPTER 10. *For All the Saints*

1. Holly Near, "Hay Una Mujer Desaparecida." Lyrics from *Imagine My Surprise! An Album of Songs about Women's Lives*, Holly Near and Ronnie Gilbert (Oakland: Redwood Records). Michelle Peña Herrarra, Nalvia Rosa Meña Alvarado, Cecilia Castro Salvadores, and Ida Amelia Almarza are four women among the thousands who "disappeared" following the United States-backed coup in Chile in 1973.

2. *The Book of Common Prayer* (New York: Church Hymnal Corp., 1979), 245.

3. *The Hymnal 1982* (New York: Church Hymnal Corporation, 1985), 287–88.

4. Holly Near, "Hay Una Mujer Desaparecida."

CHAPTER 11. *Dressed for Priesthood*

1. George Herbert, "Aaron," *The Church. The Works of George Herbert*, ed. F. E. Hutchinson (Oxford: Clarendon Press, 1941), 174. In this poem Herbert speaks of how through grace we are able to put on Christ. Through this grace we are perfected as priests.

CHAPTER 12. *Naming Evil for What It Is*

1. John Allin was Presiding Bishop of the Episcopal Church, 1974–86.

CHAPTER 15. *Crossing the River*

1. Olive Schreiner, *Dreams* (n.p., 1901), 36–37.

2. On this date eleven women were "irregularly" ordained to the priesthood in the Episcopal church in the Church of the Advocate in Philadelphia.

3. In September 1975, four more Episcopal women deacons were ordained "irregularly" to the priesthood in Washington, D.C.

4. "Christa" is the name of Edwina Sandys's sculpture of a female Christ.

5. Sue Hiatt and Jeannette Piccard were two of the eleven women ordained in Philadelphia on July 29, 1974. Ellen Barrett was the first openly lesbian woman to be ordained to the Episcopal priesthood (New York City, January, 1977). Mother Jones (1830–1930), was an Irish-American labor organizer and humanitarian.